CITYSPOTS
BELFAST

D0610317

WHAT'S IN YOUR GUIDEBOOK?

Independent authors Impartial up-to-date information from our travel experts who meticulously source local knowledge.

Experience Thomas Cook's 165 years in the travel industry and guidebook publishing enriches every word with expertise you can trust.

Travel know-how Contributions by thousands of staff around the globe, each one living and breathing travel.

Editors Travel-publishing professionals, pulling everything together to craft a perfect blend of words, pictures, maps and design.

You, the traveller We deliver a practical, no-nonsense approach to information, geared to how you really use it.

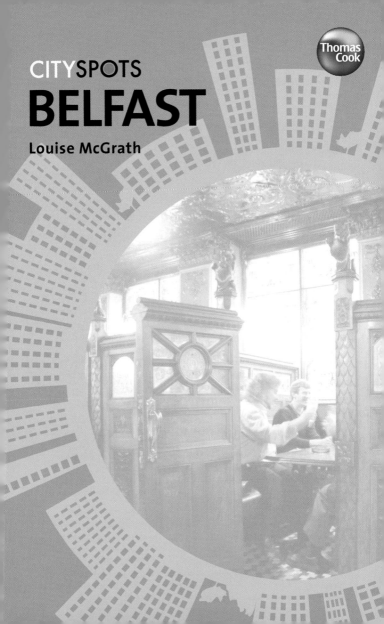

CITYSPOTS
BELFAST

Louise McGrath

Thomas Cook

Written by Louise McGrath
Cover photo (Big Fish) © Geray Sweeney/Corbis
Series design based on an original concept by Studio 183 Limited

Produced by Cambridge Publishing Management Limited
Project Editor: Rebecca McKie   Layout: Trevor Double
Maps: PC Graphics
Transport map: © Communicarta Limited

Published by Thomas Cook Publishing
A division of Thomas Cook Tour Operations Limited
Company Registration No. 1450464 England
PO Box 227, Unit 18, Coningsby Road
Peterborough PE3 8SB, United Kingdom
email: books@thomascook.com
www.thomascookpublishing.com
+ 44 (0) 1733 416477
ISBN: 978-1-84157-756-2

First edition © 2007 Thomas Cook Publishing
Text © 2007 Thomas Cook Publishing
Maps © 2007 Thomas Cook Publishing
Republic of Ireland maps: reproduced from Ordnance Survey Ireland
Permit No. 60302 © Ordnance Survey Ireland and Government of Ireland
Northern Ireland maps: reproduced by permission of the Ordnance Survey of
Northern Ireland on behalf of the Controller of Her Majesty's Stationery Office
© Crown copyright 2003 (Permit No. 60303)
Project Editor: Kelly Anne Pipes
Production/DTP: Steven Collins

Printed and bound in Spain by GraphyCems

CONTENTS

SYMBOLS KEY

The following symbols are used throughout this book:

ⓐ address ☏ telephone 🖷 fax ⓦ website address ⓔ email
🕒 opening times ⓝ public transport connections ❶ important

The following symbols are used on the maps:

🛈 information office		O	city
🛪 airport		O	large town
✚ hospital		o	small town
🕘 police station		=	motorway
🚍 bus station		—	main road
🚆 railway station		—	minor road
✝ cathedral		—	railway
❶ numbers denote featured cafés & restaurants			

Hotels and restaurants are graded by approximate price as follows:
£ budget ££ mid-range £££ expensive

▶ *The Big Fish sculpture at Donegall Quay*

Introduction

Belfast is buzzing. Not since the height of the Industrial Revolution, when it was given its city status by Queen Victoria, has it seen such a period of optimism. Today Belfast is shaking off its violent image and projecting itself as a vibrant city with plenty to offer the visitor, from art, history and green spaces to fine dining, café culture and trendy bars. Even the notorious Falls and Shankill roads are seeing a piece of the new action, with sightseeing buses and 'ex-prisoner' tours to see the political murals of West Belfast.

Belfast is the largest city in Northern Ireland, but with a population of less than 300,000 in the 2001 census, the urban area is small enough to explore easily on foot. It's also not difficult to get out of the city for a day or two if you want to head north along the stunning Antrim Coast to Giant's Causeway or south to County Down and the Mourne Mountains.

From the landmark City Hall in Donegall Square you can shop your way along Royal Avenue, over to the Cathedral Quarter and along High Street to Custom House Square. You can enjoy riverside walks along the Lagan, picnics in the Botanic Gardens and mini hikes to McArt's Fort in Cave Hill Country Park. There's interactive fun at the Odyssey complex, classical concerts at the Waterfront Hall and live bands at the Limelight. Tuck into an Ulster fry for breakfast, snack on seafood chowder and wheaten bread for lunch and sample some modern Irish cuisine for dinner, then bar hop down the Golden Mile to Botanic Avenue for some of that notorious Irish *craic*.

These days there's little to keep you away from Belfast. The new-found optimism has meant regeneration and an increase in the number of budget airlines flying to the two nearby airports. When you arrive you'll find the people warm and welcoming to visitors, keeping their identity and history firmly in sight, while looking forward with a contagious sense of enthusiasm.

● *Waterfront Hall from the river*

When to go

SEASONS & CLIMATE

Located in Belfast Lough, which leads out to the Irish Sea, Belfast has a temperate maritime climate with four distinct seasons. Cloud cover is persistent and it can generally be regarded as a damp climate with annual rainfall of 85 cm (33½in). The rain is soft and also means that green spaces stay that way throughout the summer, unlike some southern UK locations where summer sun and hosepipe bans lead to yellow, parched parks.

Summer temperatures average around 17.5°C (63.5°F) and winter temperatures about 6°C (43°F). It's best to take a raincoat

● *Crowds flock to open-air concerts at City Hall*

and/or an umbrella whenever you go, as well as something warm. Don't assume you won't need sun cream in the summer though, as the weather can surprise you.

ANNUAL EVENTS
March
St Patrick's Day (17 March); the first major event of the year. It wasn't until 1998 that Belfast started having its own city centre celebrations for Ireland's patron saint, including concerts by renowned musicians such as Shane McGowan on stage outside the City Hall. In 2006, the carnival moved to Custom House Square. After the carnival event, plenty head straight to the pub for all-day drinking, jollity and traditional music in bars such as Fibber McGee's (see page 75).

April
Between the Lines (BTL) is a literary festival with readings and workshops with local and international authors at the Crescent Arts Centre, ⓦ www.crescentarts.org. Later in the month the Cathedral Quarter Arts Festival sees fringe theatre and performing arts groups, as well as music, comedy, film, circus acts and visual arts events take over arts venues and pubs, ⓦ www.cqaf.com

May
The Balmoral Show at the Balmoral Showground is Ireland's largest agricultural show, featuring a children's farm, dog agility competitions, falconry displays, livestock, Pony Club games, sheep shearing, showjumping and gun dog displays, as well as other entertainment from music to circus. ⓦ www.balmoralshow.co.uk

July

On 12 July, the Orange Order celebrates the victory of William of Orange over James I in 1690 with 'demonstrations'. The Belfast demonstrations are the largest in Northern Ireland and see Orange Order flute bands parading through the city centre and south to Edenderry Field for speeches.

Later in the month, the Beat Summer Carnival is a cross-community event in Custom House Square with a carnival parade, floats, bands, dancers and cultural groups from a diverse section of the community. Ⓦ www.belfastcarnival.org

Belfast International Rose Trials and Rose Week at Sir Thomas and Lady Dixon Park attracts 50,000 visitors for the serious rose competition as well as fun activities for children from face-painting to treasure hunts.

August

Belfast Pride sees a week of arts and culture events culminating in a colourful parade through the city centre, Ⓦ www.belfastpride.com. Also in August is the West Belfast Festival – Féile an Phobail, the largest community-led festival in Europe, with internationally renowned musicians, exhibitions, debates, drama events, an international food fair and a parade. Ⓦ www.feilebelfast.com

September

Ireland's largest arts festival comes to Belfast Festival at Queen's each year with an impressive programme of events featuring renowned and up-and-coming performers and artists, cutting-edge performances and special projects in theatre, dance,

music, visual art, film and spoken word throughout the city.
Ⓦ www.belfastfestival.com

October
From the end of September through to October, the Cathedral
Quarter celebrates Open House Festival, traditional arts with a
focus on music events from Irish traditional to bluegrass, Cajun
and country. Ⓦ www.openhousefestival.com

November
Book lovers flock to the Wellington Park Hotel on the Malone
Road for the country's biggest and longest-running book fair,
with dozens of dealers doing a good trade in second-hand, rare
and antiquarian publications. November also sees the
CineMagic World Screen Festival for Young People, with
screenings throughout the city. Ⓦ www.cinemagic.org.uk

PUBLIC HOLIDAYS
New Year's Day 1 Jan
St Patrick's Day 17 March
Good Friday Friday before Easter Sunday, Mar/Apr
Easter Monday Monday after Easter Sunday, Mar/April
May Bank Holiday first Monday in May
Spring Bank Holiday last Monday in May
Battle of the Boyne 12 July
August Bank Holiday last Monday in August
Christmas Day 25 Dec
Boxing Day 26 Dec

Rebirth of Belfast

The new optimism felt in Belfast since the Good Friday
Agreement has resonated throughout the city, attracting
investment into run-down areas. The first 'new builds' included
the BT Tower, Hilton Hotel and apartments on Laganside, plus
the landmark Odyssey Complex and Science Park which have
made inroads into the Titanic Quarter.

The redevelopment of the former Gasworks 'brown site' into
a landscaped showpiece with offices, the Radisson Hotel,
housing and cafés has been hailed as a major success. Custom
House Square has also had a makeover, giving it new life and
opening it up to live events and festivals. The Grand Opera
House has been extended and improved, and the former Ulster
Bank in the Cathedral Quarter has been transformed into the
elegant Merchant Hotel.

The regeneration and construction that has already taken
place is just the beginning. Over the next two decades the
Titanic Quarter is to be transformed into a new maritime
quarter, adding cafés and bars, retail space, apartments, hotel
and office buildings, as well as a new quay at Abercorn Basin,
community facilities, and public art and event spaces.

In 2008 the £320m retail development Victoria Square by
Cornmarket is due to open with dozens of high-street stores.
Laganside is to see further regeneration, turning it into a vibrant
nightlife and entertainment area, plus the construction of Obel
Tower at Donegall Quay, set to be Northern Ireland's tallest building.

The Ulster Museum (due for completion in 2009) undergoes
a rejuvenation which includes a new entrance and arrival space,

improved history and natural science galleries and a new rooftop gallery, plus a new café and restaurant. The Cathedral Quarter is also earmarked for a £10m replacement building for the Old Museum Arts Centre on a site behind St Anne's Cathedral.

The city centre was a virtual no-go area at night before the Good Friday Agreement. While the political future is still being defined, construction and regeneration of the city has made its residents feel a sense of renewal. Property prices have been booming, and tourists feel happier to visit, with Belfast becoming one of the hottest city-break destinations in Great Britain.

⬤ *Regeneration continues to transform the city centre*

History

Belfast's name derives from the Gaelic *Béal Feirste*, meaning 'sandy ford at the mouth of the River Farset'. The location of the Farset, now contained within a pipe under High Street, is the oldest part of the city: John de Courcy built a castle here in the 12th century; in 1611 Baron Arthur Chichester built another on the same site, which was destroyed in a fire in 1708.

Chichester encouraged the plantation of Ulster by English and Scottish Protestant Planters, but during the Irish Uprising of 1641, thousands of these Planters were massacred, and many fled back to England. James II became King of Ireland in 1685 but the arrival of William of Orange saw support by Ulster, where there was a Protestant majority. James was defeated in 1690 and penal laws were brought in, curbing the rights of Catholics.

By the early 18th century, Belfast was a large settlement, the arrival of French Huguenots stimulating the growth of the linen industry. One of their descendents, the philanthropist and radical Henry Joy McCracken, formed the United Irishmen with Theobold Wolfe Tone. Their aim was to end oppressive English rule, but following their 1798 rebellion at the Battle of Antrim, McCracken was captured and hanged.

During the 19th century the Industrial Revolution led to growth in shipbuilding, ropeworks, tobacco factories and linen mills, and Belfast receiving city status by royal decree. With new employment opportunities and the devastating effects of the Potato Famine in rural areas, people flooded into the city, settling in areas that were already predominantly either Catholic or Protestant. Unrest continued into the new century, and following the Irish War of

Independence, most of Ulster saw partition from the South and the creation of Northern Ireland with Belfast as its capital.

The city continued to grow, becoming the world's most important shipbuilding location. However, Belfast was severely bombed during World War II, and the post-war period saw jobs drying up as air travel began to supersede sea travel.

Old religious prejudices led to Civil Rights marches by Catholics and riots by Loyalist gangs, culminating in the British Army's deployment to keep the peace in 1969. Direct Rule by the British Government replaced the Northern Ireland government and the period known as The Troubles continued for almost 30 years, with violence by the IRA, loyalist UVF and other paramilitary groups. After peace talks with republican party Sinn Féin, and an IRA ceasefire, the Good Friday Agreement was put into place in 1998, leading to the creation of the Northern Ireland Assembly. However this was suspended by the British Government in 2002.

● Queen's University, built in prosperous Victorian times

Lifestyle

In the past decade the city centre has undergone a physical transformation and the lifestyle of many of Belfast's residents has also improved. The city centre is now open and vibrant with a booming café culture, new bars, restaurants, shops and cultural venues. Even the Falls and Shankill roads have become attractions as tourists take guided tours to see the political murals, something that would have seemed unlikely as little as a decade ago. Despite this, the political future remains uncertain and with The Troubles still in the memories of most of the population, old rivalries and fears persist.

Many children still go to Catholic or Protestant schools and therefore identity is defined by community, with sports, music, language, and even the football team you support defined by your education and religion. Growing numbers of integrated schools and cross-community projects are working tirelessly to promote mutual understanding and transcend these rivalries.

In the Cathedral Quarter, city centre and South Belfast you really have a feel of this transformation, an excitement about the changes and the benefits of a newly affluent society. Students from both communities meet at college and begin to understand each other, while equal opportunities at work have also led to further integration and tolerance.

While there is still a long way to go and some issues may never be resolved, Belfast is buzzing. People enjoy the same lifestyle as those in the rest of the UK, working and playing hard, particularly now they can freely go out after work in the city centre to enjoy the new generation of restaurants, fringe theatre and bars, plus late-night shopping on a Thursday and drinking down the Golden Mile on a Friday. The cost of living is more or less the same as the rest of the UK, but you might find that bars, restaurants and hotels are cheaper than in London.

Most people are happy to show visitors round their city, but just be careful about being over pertinent about politics and religion, as it is a sensitive subject, and avoid wearing football shirts that might attract negative attention. Let them show you the murals or talk about their personal views and orientations if they like, otherwise take in the history at the museums and on the tour bus, and enjoy a large helping of the *craic* at the pub.

🔺 *Belfast pub culture is thriving*

Culture

The official language of the Republic of Ireland, the Irish language or Gaelic (Gaeilge) is recognised as their native language by a large percentage of the nationalist community. It's taught in Catholic schools as well as at the Gaelic language centre in the Falls Road, Cultúrlann MacAdam O'Fiaich (see page 87). The church is the hub of the community for Catholic residents and is what has united them throughout The Troubles. Not only do Catholics come to pray together, but the church is a meeting point for dance and music groups, where children (and adults) can learn traditional Irish dancing and how to play instruments heard in traditional Irish music, including the fiddle, mandolin, *bodhrán* and tin whistle. Gaelic football and hurling clubs are also affiliated round the church (see page 35). You often know when you're in a Catholic or Nationalist neighbourhood as many of the shop signs will be in Celtic script or even in Irish. You can see dancing on St Patrick's Day and in arts centres. The best place to hear traditional music is in pubs such as Fibber McGee's and The Rotterdam. Celtic art is shown in arts centres and the Gaelic language centre and you can buy it from the WickerMan in Donegall Arcade.

Other cultural forms have developed in spite of the turbulent politics, particularly with the investment into new arts centres and venues such as the Waterfront Hall. Home to the Ulster Orchestra, this is also one of the main places to see classical music and opera. Opera can also be seen outside Belfast at the National Trust Castle Ward estate in Strangford during June with productions by the specially formed Castle Ward Opera.

New artists and new galleries are springing up. The Ulster Museum puts on a good range of temporary exhibitions but other places include the Linen Hall Library, Catalyst Arts (see page 67), Crescent Arts Centre and the Naughton Gallery at Queen's (see page 98).

◆ *The 2,250-seater auditorium at Waterfront Hall*

THE HAMELY TONGUE

As part of the Good Friday Agreement, it was agreed that 'respect and understanding and tolerance' would be given to the Ulster-Scots language. Also known as Ullans, Ulster-Scots is a variant of Scots that developed among the descendents of the Planters from Scotland since the 16th century and is spoken by an estimated 100,000 people in Northern Ireland. It was actually recognised as a language back in 1992. The Ulster Scots Agency promotes the study, development and use of the language and culture by publishing encouraging contemporary writing and providing teaching resources for schools. Speaking of the language has also meant a rise in other cultural forms associated with the Ulster Scots peoples, including music and literature. Many Ulster Scots events take place in Orange Halls. See the Ulster Scots Agency website for a list of upcoming events.

Ⓦ www.ulsterscotsagency.com

▶ *Albert Square from the river*

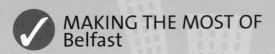

Shopping

WHERE TO SHOP

Belfast has plenty of opportunities for shopping and spending your hard-earned cash. The city centre is the main destination with high-street stores along Donegall Place leading into Royal Avenue and the streets off it, especially Donegall Square North, Wellington Place, Upper Queen Street and Howard Street to the west, and Rosemary Street, Bridge Street, Castle Place, Cornmarket, Arthur Street, William Street and Ann Street to the east side. Marks and Spencer can be found at the bottom of Donegall Place, Bhs on Castle Place, Dunnes Stores along Cornmarket and Debenhams in CastleCourt Shopping Centre.

CastleCourt is presently the largest shopping centre in the city with 60 local and international shops over two storeys, a choice of eateries on the upper floor and plenty of parking at the back. The Spires Mall on Wellington Street has a dozen or so shops, as does Donegall Arcade on Castle Place. A large project is underway in the city to build the new Victoria Square retail and leisure outlet, due for completion in 2008, with promises of many more high-street names moving into the city. In West Belfast, Andersonstown shopping centre is the best place to go for Gaelic sports strip.

For designer shopping you need to go to the Lisburn Road where you'll find the likes of Emporio Armani, Helen McAlinden, Bisón, Marina Rinaldi, Space NK, La Cucina Cookshop and many more.

Out of town there's good high-street shopping in Lisburn town centre and a large Marks and Spencer at Sprucefield

🔺 *Celtic souvenirs at the WickerMan*

MARKETS

There are two main markets in Belfast city centre, namely the 19th-century St George's Market on Oxford Street, with a mixed market on Friday and the City Food & Garden Market on Saturday, and Smithfield Market on West Street/ Winetavern Street, a daily (except Sunday) market selling a little of everything. You'll find a good selection of local breads at Saturday's food stalls at St George's. There'll also be a wide selection of other locally produced goods here, including cider, ham and goats' cheese.

nearby. In Antrim, you'll find the Junction One factory outlet centre with everything from Adidas to Toyzone bargains.

WHAT TO BUY

There are plenty of places to buy gifts and souvenirs, but shop around. Possibly the best place is the WickerMan in Donegall Arcade, which has a wide selection of Celtic arts and crafts. Also try the Belfast Welcome Centre, which sells the more standardised souvenirs, cards and maps, and the shops at the Ulster Museum and other attractions. Buy high-street fashion in the city centre, designer clothes in the Lisburn Road and bag a bargain at Junction One, 20 miles out of town in Antrim.

Eating & drinking

There's little chance of avoiding an Ulster fry when you visit Belfast, although since it features mostly sausages, bacon and black or white pudding (along with soda bread, potato farls, fried eggs and sometimes mushrooms), vegetarians might be a bit put off. These days there are a few more vegetarian options, including plenty of cereals and some smoothie bars, but you'll need to shop around. Once you're set up with a good breakfast you'll not be wanting for anything for quite some time, and most locals usually grab a sandwich or light lunch. There are plenty of coffee shops and snack bars opening where you can have a doorstep sandwich, soup and wheaten bread or two-course lunch specials. Lunch is generally called 'dinner' and after work you go home for your 'tea', although plenty of people stay out in the city centre after work and there are lots of dining options.

In the restaurants you'll find traditional dishes such as Irish stew (once made from mutton but today from lamb, carrots and onions), sausage and champ (creamy mashed potato with scallions – spring onions), and boiled bacon (ham) and cabbage. There's usually plenty of meat on the menu, including succulent plates of Irish beef, pork and lamb. You also can't miss the fresh fish and seafood with warm bowls of seafood chowder and

RESTAURANT CATEGORIES
Price ratings in this book are based on the average price of a two-course meal for one without drinks.
£ under 15   ££ 15–25   £££ over £25

wheaten bread, fresh prawns, herrings, mackerel, lobster, oysters and mussels from the sea and freshwater fish such as salmon and trout. As you head up the Antrim Coast or south towards Strangford Lough and the Mournes, you'll find a greater selection of fish on the menu.

Instead of spending a fortune in the restaurants you can also opt for a picnic, if the weather is good. Pick up some bread, cheese and ham from St George's market and head out to the parks from City Hall and Botanic to Cave Hill and Colin Glen.

Bread plays an important part in the Belfast diet with potato bread (made from mashed potato), soda farls (raised with bicarbonate of soda rather than yeast), barm brack (fruit soda, a traditional bread to eat toasted on Halloween), boxty (made from potato, flour, egg and bicarb and said to have emerged during the potato famine), plain loaf (white sliced bread) and the good old crusty Belfast bap (bread roll). You'll see bread served with your Ulster fry, soups and chowder, in sandwiches and toasted with butter. The high level of milk production in Northern Ireland means plenty of dairy products from creamy fresh butter to strong hard cheese. Look out for locally produced goats' milk and cheese too – you'll be able to pick some up at St George's Market.

○ *Apartment: one of the hippest eateries in town (see page 71)*

With all that bread you'll need to wash it down with a few drinks. Tea is very popular here, with buttered wheaten or toasted barm brack, and you'll want to try the famous Irish coffee, but in the end there's no excuse needed to head out for a few jars.

The most famous Irish drink is Guinness which is drunk plentifully in Belfast, but cider is also a popular drink. Armagh is known as the orchard county and you might pick up some homemade cider in the organic market, but in the pubs the cider is from the South. Known as Bulmer's (not to be confused with the English Bulmer's) in the South, in Northern Ireland and the rest of the UK it is marketed as Magners. There has been a huge surge in sales in the past few years and you'll see plenty of large bottles (or draft) sold. Drink it in a pint glass with plenty of ice – they say it helps re-hydrate you! If that's not enough, finish with a few drams of Bushmills Irish Whiskey as a nightcap.

A RESTAURANT REVOLUTION

The development of the city centre has led to the development of a modern Irish cuisine, spearheaded by celebrity chefs such as Paul Rankin, Michael Deane and Robbie Millar (who, sadly, was killed in a car accident in 2005). What makes the food modern is the variation on traditional dishes or an international twist with Asian, Mediterranean, Latin American or other influences in the ingredients. Expect dishes such as crispy Mexican black bean dumplings and Strangford crab linguini from Rankin, and steak & Guinness pie with flaky pastry or smoked haddock and creamed leeks from Deane.

Entertainment & nightlife

Socialising plays a big part in Belfast life, from dinner and drinks to a full-on pub crawl, theatre and classical orchestras to traditional Irish music and fringe performing arts groups. There are no rules on where and when you should go out, except the licensing laws, although these too have relaxed in some areas, with some pubs staying open until midnight at the weekends and clubs until 02.00 or 03.00. Evening films usually start between 18.00 and 21.00, concerts and shows around 20.00 and gigs around 21.00.

At the Belfast Welcome Centre (or in your hotel) you can pick up a copy of *Whatabout*, which has listings for music and entertainment, pubs and clubs, theatre, opera and comedy, as well as family entertainment, shopping, eating and attractions. Also look out for a copy of *FATE*, which gives a round-up on the coolest bars, clubs, fashion and music.

BARS & CLUBS
For gentle, up-market bars, stay in the Cathedral Quarter, city centre and South Belfast, where hotel bars offer snacks and evening drinks, sometimes with music. There is a new crop of bars for the more mature and discerning crowd, including the likes of Café Vaudeville in Donegall Square South. If you want something more down to earth, head to the Golden Mile, where pubs from Robinson's and The Crown down to Shaftesbury Square offer lively nights. Students and younger crowds also hang out in Botanic and Ormeau, where you'll find plenty of busy bars and pubs. The trendier crowd hang out in bars along

the Lisburn Road. For clubbing, you're pretty much talking about the same areas, along Ormeau Avenue, Botanic Avenue, Shaftesbury Square and Cathedral Quarter around Donegall Street. For gay bars try Kremlin in Donegall Street and Mynt in Dunbar Street, both in the Cathedral Quarter.

🔺 *You're never far from a good pint in Belfast*

MUSIC

There's no shortage of music in Belfast, with something for everyone. Pick up the free listings magazines (see page 30) and take your pick. You can hear classical music and opera at the Waterfront Hall along with big-name concerts. The Ulster

⬥ *Fibber McGee's hosts regular gigs*

Orchestra and jazz groups play at the Ulster Hall in Bedford Street. The best places to catch the latest bands are The Limelight and Spring & Airbrake (Ormeau Avenue) and the Mandela Hall (in Queen's University). You can hear live traditional music in Fibber McGee's (Brunswick Street), The Rotterdam (Pilot Street), The John Hewitt (Donegall Street), The Fountain Bar (Fountain Street) and Cultúrlann in the Falls Road, among others. During the warmer months there are open-air concerts outside the City Hall, in Custom House Square and in Botanic Gardens.

THEATRE
The only full-time producing theatre in Northern Ireland is the Lyric Theatre, Ⓦ www.lyrictheatre.co.uk, but there are fringe arts centres such as Catalyst Arts, Ⓦ www.catalystarts.org.uk, Crescent Arts, Ⓦ www.crescentarts.org and Old Museum Arts Centre, Ⓦ www.oldmuseumartscentre.org, where you can see innovative new artists and productions.

CINEMA
The Queen's Film Theatre, Ⓦ www.queensfilmtheatre.com, shows a wide range of films in their original language with subtitles – screenings usually start between 18.00 and 21.00. Your hotel, the Belfast Welcome Centre or the venue (on University Square) should have a free booklet with the latest listings. Other Belfast cinemas include the Movie Houses on Dublin Road and Yorkgate, the Strand in Hollywood Road, Cineplex Belfast on the Falls road and the Vue and Sheridan Imax at the Odyssey Centre.

Sport & relaxation

SPECTATOR SPORTS

Football

The Carnegie Premier League is the main NI league but it doesn't carry the same prestige as the leagues in England, Scotland and the rest of Europe. One of Belfast's main teams is Linfield FC, based at Windsor Park, which is also the venue for the Northern Ireland team's international matches. ⓐ Windsor Park, Donegall Avenue ⓦ Carnegie Premier League: http://irishpremierleague.com, ⓦ Irish Football Association: www.irishfa.com

◔ Catch great rugby at Ravenshill

Gaelic Football

Gaelic football, a cross between football and rugby, is hugely popular among the Catholic community, with teams affiliated to church parishes. County Antrim trains and holds its home games at Casement Park in the Falls Road. It's a tough game but very entertaining to watch. ⓐ Anderstown Road ⓦ GAA: www.gaa.ie

Horseracing

Northern Ireland's premier racecourse is Down Royal Racecourse at Downpatrick. There are regular fixtures throughout the year and tickets are available online. ⓐ 24 Ballyduggan Road, Downpatrick ⓦ www.downroyal.com

Hurling

Like Gaelic football, hurling teams are affiliated to the local parishes. Casement Park is the venue for County Antrim team home games. ⓐ Anderstown Road ⓦ GAA: www.gaa.ie

Ice Hockey

The Belfast Giants are the major team in the city and their home is at the Odyssey Arena, where home Elite League games are played against other UK teams. ⓐ Odyssey Arena, Queen's Quay ⓦ Belfast Giants: www.belfastgiants.co.uk

Rugby

Ravenhill Stadium is home to Ulster Rugby, which has stayed in the Irish Rugby Football Union since partition in 1921, meaning six of the nine counties of the Ulster branch are in Northern Ireland and three are in the Republic of Ireland. So you can expect to see games against Leinster, Munster and Connacht, as well as teams from Scotland, England and Wales. ❸ Ravenhill Stadium, Ravenhill ⓦ Ulster Rugby: www.ulsterrugby.ie

PARTICIPATION SPORTS

Belfast has numerous sports centres run by the city council, as well as private gyms and health clubs, including LA Fitness, ⓦ www.lafitness.co.uk, LivingWell Health Club, ⓦ www.livingwell.com and Fitness First, ⓦ www.fitnessfirst.co.uk

Golf

Northern Ireland is a popular destination for golf and there are several courses within easy reach of Belfast, including Carrickfergus Golf Club, ⓦ www.bentra.co.uk, Hilton Templepatrick Golf Club, ⓦ www.hilton.co.uk, Royal Belfast Golf Club in Holywood, ⓦ www.royalbelfast.com, and Royal County Down in Newcastle, ⓦ www.royalcountydown.org

Outdoors and adventure sports

Close to Belfast you can go walking in Colin Glen Forest Park, ⓦ www.colinglentrust.org, along the Lagan Towpath to Lisburn (see page 91) or in Cave Hill Country Park (see page 82). For longer treks head to the Glens of Antrim (see pages 121–2) or the Mourne Mountains (see page 110). In the Mournes you can also go climbing and orienteering, with courses at Tollymore Mountain Centre, ⓦ www.tollymore.com. Blue Lough Mountain and Watersports Centre run adventure days plus courses and practice days in canoeing, climbing, bouldering, campcraft, mountain biking and much more, ⓦ www.mountainandwater.com

Accommodation

In general, accommodation in Belfast costs around the same as in other parts of the UK, but there's quite a variety of places to stay, and with the city's booming development, new hotels are opening quite regularly. It's best to book somewhere in advance. The tourist office website has a 'special deals' section as well as full listings of other accommodation according to classification, ⓦ www.gotobelfast.com. Also try the Northern Ireland Tourist Board, ⓦ www.visitnorthernireland.com and Tourism Ireland, ⓦ www.discoverireland.com. There are several websites offering online bookings, often with discounts; some of the best include ⓦ www.goireland.com, www.expedia.co.uk, www.hotels.com, www.hotelclub.com and www.hini.org.uk

If you find yourself in Belfast without anywhere to stay, the staff in the Belfast Welcome Centre in Donegall Place are very helpful. Alternatively, try some of the suggestions below according to your taste and budget.

The best places to stay are in the city centre along the streets around Donegall Square, along Great Victoria Street to Shaftesbury Square, Botanic, Stranmillis and Malone in South Belfast. There are some large hotels such as the Hilton, by the Waterfront Hall, and the Radisson in the old Gasworks south of

> **PRICE RATING**
> Gradings used in this book are based on the average price for a double room per night, including breakfast.
> £ under £60   ££ £60–£100   £££ over £100

St George's Market, and new places are opening in the Cathedral Quarter. You can find places to stay in other parts of Belfast, including along the Antrim Road in North Belfast, Dunmurry in West Belfast and Stormont in East Belfast, but for easy access to attractions it's easier and safer to stay more centrally. For out-of-town options, see the relevant chapters or the websites on the previous page. Accommodation tends to be divided into the following categories:

Travelodge Belfast Central £ Reasonably priced hotel with a breakfast option, located within crawling distance of Fibber McGee's and other lively pubs. ⓐ 15 Brunswick Street ⓣ 0870 1 911687 ⓦ www.travelodge.co.uk ⓝ Bus: Europa Buscentre

Benedict's ££ Located at the top end of Belfast's Golden Mile, this trendy hotel has a themed bar, live DJs and music, and slick guestrooms in modern décor. ⓐ 7–21 Bradbury Place, Shaftesbury Square ⓣ 028 9059 1999 ⓦ www. benedictshotel.co.uk ⓔ info@benedictshotel.co.uk ⓝ Bus: 8A, 7B

Days Hotel ££ Northern Ireland's largest hotel, with spacious and comfortable guestrooms. Located just off the Golden Mile near Europa Buscentre. ⓐ 40 Hope Street ⓣ 028 9024 2494 ⓦ www.dayshotelbelfast.com ⓝ Bus: Europa Buscentre, Train: Great Victoria Street

Holiday Inn Belfast ££ Located in the heart of Belfast's Golden Mile with contemporary rooms, restaurant and bar.

🅐 22 Ormeau Avenue 🅣 0870 400 9005 🅕 028 9062 6546
🅦 www.belfast.holiday-inn.com 🅔 belfast@ichotelsgroup.com
🚆 Train: Great Victoria Street

Lansdowne Hotel ££ Located close to Cave Hill and Belfast
Castle with easy access out of town towards the Antrim Coast,
this contemporary hotel has a restaurant, karaoke on Fridays
and live music at the weekends. 🅐 657 Antrim Road 🅣 028 9077
3317 🅦 www.welcome-group.co.uk 🅔 info@the-lansdowne.co.uk
🚌 Bus: 1A-E

🔺 *The Europa Hotel: in the heart of the city*

Madison's ££ Stylish small hotel with bar, restaurant and club, this is a favourite with rock bands and is located in the heart of lively Botanic. ⓐ 59–63 Botanic Avenue ⓣ 028 9050 9800 ⓕ 028 9050 9808 ⓦ www.madisonshotel.com ⓝ Bus: 7A-B, 8A-B

Stormont Hotel ££ Overlooks the Northern Ireland government grounds and has two restaurants. ⓐ Upper Newtownards Road ⓣ 028 9065 6621 ⓕ 028 9048 0240 ⓦ www.hastingshotels.com ⓔ res@stor.hastingshotels.com ⓝ Bus: 20A

The Crescent Townhouse Hotel £££ Intimate and stylish hotel located in the heart of the cool Botanic area, with canopy beds and Victorian-style roll-top baths, plus a brasserie and bar. ⓐ 13 Lower Crescent ⓣ 028 9032 3349 ⓦ www.crescenttownhouse.com ⓝ Bus: 9A-B, 8A-B

Europa Hotel £££ Renowned as 'the most bombed hotel in Europe', but don't worry – that dates back to The Troubles. Today it is one of the best hotels in the city, located next to the Grand Opera House and opposite the Crown Liquor Saloon. ⓐ Great Victoria Street ⓣ 028 9027 1066 ⓕ 028 9032 7800 ⓦ www.hastings hotels.com ⓝ Bus: Europa Buscentre

Hilton Belfast £££ Located next to the Waterfront Hall, this 5-star hotel has restaurants, bars, riverside views and a health club. ⓐ 4 Lanyon Place ⓣ 028 9027 7000 ⓕ 028 9027 7277 ⓦ www.hilton.co.uk/belfast ⓔ reservations.belfast@hilton.com ⓝ Bus: Laganside Buscentre

Malmaison £££ Stylish and slinky guestrooms or rock 'n' roll suites with CD players and city views, plus a trendy brasserie and bar downstairs. ⓐ 34–38 Victoria Street ⓣ 028 9022 0210 ⓦ www.malmaison-belfast.com ⓔ belfast@malmaison.com ⓝ Bus: Donegall Square/Royal Avenue

Radisson SAS Hotel Belfast £££ Modern, comfortable hotel with restaurant, bar and large car park. ⓐ The Gasworks, Cromac Place ⓣ 028 9043 4065 ⓦ www.radisson.com ⓝ Bus: 77, 30

Ten Square Boutique Hotel £££ Chic, central boutique hotel with Asian-style guestrooms, low-level beds and rich cream carpets. ⓐ 10 Donegall Square South ⓣ 028 9024 1001 ⓦ www.tensquare.co.uk ⓔ reservations@tensquare.co.uk ⓝ Bus: Donegall Square

YOUTH HOSTELS

Arnies Backpackers £ Located near Queen's University, you'll be near all the nightlife and won't have to pay a packet. ⓐ 63 Fitzwilliam Street ⓣ 028 9024 2867 ⓦ www.arniesbackpackers.co.uk ⓔ info@arniesbackpackers.co.uk ⓝ Bus: 8A-B

Belfast International Youth Hostel £ Located right on Belfast's Golden Mile, this hostel is well located for sightseeing and going out. ⓐ 22–32 Donegall Road ⓣ 028 9032 4733 ⓦ www.hini.org.uk ⓔ info@hini.org.uk ⓝ Bus: 8A, 7B

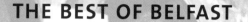

THE BEST OF BELFAST

There's a lot to see and do in Belfast but if you've only got a few hours or days to spare, try some of the following must-sees.

TOP 10 ATTRACTIONS

- **City Bus Tour** A good introduction to Belfast, covering the city centre and nearby attractions (see page 61).

- **City Hall** The city centre's most prominent landmark: see the elaborate interior or picnic in the gardens (see page 65).

- **Ulster Museum** A treasure trove of history, science and art, giving a thorough insight into Northern Ireland's past and present (see page 99).

- **Crown Liquor Saloon** One of the oldest and most elaborate bars in the city – sit in a 'snug' with a pint of Guinness (see page 66).

- **Shopping spree** Pick up organic goodies at St George's Market, Celtic souvenirs from the Wicker Man and designer labels in the Lisburn Road (see pages 24–5).

- **Concert at Waterfront Hall** Belfast's primary concert hall hosts the Ulster Orchestra plus opera and comedy (see page 69).

- **West Belfast Murals** Take a guided tour or take in the political murals at your own pace (see pages 86–7).

- **Belfast Titanic walking trail** Hear anecdotes about the city centre from the City Hall and Albert Clock to the Titanic (see page 90).

- **W5 at Odyssey** An interactive discovery centre with scientific experiments, creative challenges and feats of physical strength (see page 94).

- **Night out** Bar hop down the Golden Mile – start in the city centre and head towards Shaftesbury Square and Botanic (see pages 72–5).

◆ *The opulent Crown Liquor Saloon*

HALF-DAY: BELFAST IN A HURRY

If you've only a few hours free, pick up Irish crafts from the WickerMan in Donegall Arcade then hop on a Belfast City Sightseeing bus tour. In 90 minutes you'll get a flavour of the city centre, Cathedral Quarter, Titanic Quarter, West Belfast murals, University District and Golden Mile/nightlife. If you've time left, jump off at the Europa Hotel and cross the road to the Crown Liquor Saloon for a pint.

1 DAY: TIME TO SEE A LITTLE MORE

If you've got a whole day, take the bus tour in the morning, stop for lunch in the Crown Liquor Saloon, then explore the city centre on foot. Take a free tour round City Hall and take a peek at the rich collection of Irish books in the Linen Hall. If you've time, wander up Royal Avenue to buy souvenirs in the Belfast Welcome Centre or at the Wicker Man in Donegall Arcade.

2–3 DAYS: SHORT CITY BREAK

This gives you time to explore beyond the city centre. Depending on your interests, take the above, opt for a walking tour with ex-political prisoners through West Belfast or the multi-media Belfast Titanic Trail to discover sites in the city associated with the Titanic story. If the weather is good, spend the day out of town at the Ulster Folk & Transport Museum. There should also be time for an afternoon's shopping along Royal Avenue and CastleCourt and a night out at the Vaudeville Café for jazz and cocktails, Robinson's and Fibber McGee's for traditional Irish music or Botanic Avenue for a more student vibe.

LONGER: ENJOYING BELFAST TO THE FULL

If you've more than a couple of days on your hands, take your hire car or book an organised tour outside the city. Some of the best days out include a drive along the stunning Antrim Coast to Giant's Causeway and Bushmills Whiskey Distillery, a day in Downpatrick visiting the Cathedral, St Patrick's Visitor Centre, Down County Museum, Armagh City and Navan Fort or walking in the Mourne Mountains and a fish dinner in Newcastle or Dundrum.

⬧ Bus tours take in all the sights

Something for nothing

You don't have to spend a fortune getting to know Belfast as there are plenty of free or fairly cheap activities to keep you occupied. Your first stop should be the Belfast Welcome Centre where information, advice, maps and brochures are all free.

Start by exploring the city centre on foot. Tours of City Hall and browsing the superb collection of books at the Linen Hall library don't cost a penny. Take in top attractions such as the Albert Clock, Custom House Square, Lagan Lookout, Europa Hotel, Grand Opera House and Crown Liquor Saloon (see pages 60–75). Then head south along Victoria Street to see the impressive Queens University and on to the Ulster Museum (see pages 95–9).

If you're good on your feet head up the Falls Road, with its numerous political murals, and pop into Cultúrlann MacAdam, the Irish language and culture centre, where you can stop for a café lunch, hear locals speaking Gaelic and have a browse in the bookshop (see page 87).

To see loyalist political murals and get a taster for Ulster-Scots culture, head up the Shankill Road to visit Fernhill House (The People's Museum), which costs next to nothing, and learn about life in the Shankill area from the 19th century to the present. Look out for the statue of King Billy that tops the West Belfast Orange Hall at Carlisle Circus (see pages 86).

On a good day, walk or cycle along the Lagan towpath, which runs 10 miles from Stranmillis in South Belfast to Lisburn in County Down (see page 91). The route runs along the riverbank through beautiful scenery, urban parkland and nature trails.

If that's too far, then head for one of the city parks, including Botanic Gardens for its impressive plant collections and relaxing lawns (see page 91), Cave Hill Country Park for Belfast Castle and panoramic city views (see page 82), the Japanese Garden at Sir Thomas and Lady Dixon Park or Ormeau Park for woodland and wildlife (see page 95).

🔺 *The Linen Hall Library: fascinating and free*

When it rains

The likelihood of it raining when you're in Belfast is quite high, so you should really just take a raincoat and an umbrella and not let a few drops of rain stop you from enjoying the sights outdoors. The open-top buses are swapped for ones with roofs on rainy days, so you can still take a tour round the city. The same goes for black taxi tours, but if you really want to get out of the rain, there's no shortage of options.

Take a tour round City Hall (see page 65), which will take about an hour, and takes in the grand staircase, oak council chamber, the ornate dome and other features of this Classical Renaissance building. You can spend several hours in the Ulster Museum (see page 99), which has something for everyone including art, archaeology, local history and natural science, plus special exhibitions.

The Odyssey Centre is an all-day option (especially good if you have children with you) and you can park the car there if you have one. Spend the morning getting hands-on in W5, an interactive centre of discovery (see page 94), then have lunch in the Odyssey Pavilion before seeing a film at the IMAX cinema in the afternoon. You might even be able to catch a game by the Belfast Giants ice hockey team, if you're lucky.

There are several indoor shopping options, the largest of which is the CastleCourt Shopping Centre, where you've everything you need to keep you fed, watered and clothed for the day.

If the rain carries on into the evening, take in a film at the Queen's Film Theatre, classical music at the Waterfront Hall or performing arts at the Crescent Arts Centre (see page 98). Of course you could also take refuge in one of the many public houses from the Crown Liquor Saloon, Robinson's and Fibber McGee's to The Rotterdam or Lavery's, by which time the rain should have stopped or you'll be too full of the 'black stuff' to care!

🔺 *CastleCourt Shopping Centre: no umbrella needed*

On arrival

TIME DIFFERENCES

Belfast follows Greenwich Mean Time (GMT). During Daylight Saving Time (last Sunday in March to last Sunday in October), the clocks are put ahead 1 hour – British Summer Time (BST).

In the Belfast summer, at 12.00 noon, time at home is as follows:

Australia: Eastern Standard Time 21.00, Central Standard Time 20.30, Western Standard Time 19.00

New Zealand: 23.00

South Africa: 13.00

UK: 12.00 noon

USA: Eastern Time 07.00, Central Time 06.00, Mountain Time 05.00, Pacific Time 04.00, Alaska 03.00.

ARRIVING

By air

Belfast has two airports: Belfast International Airport and George Best Belfast City Airport. The international airport is located 18 miles northwest of the city and is Northern Ireland's busiest airport. Facilities include shops and restaurants, bureaux de change, postal services, cash machines, airport information, Business Lounge and baby changing facilities.

The blue and white Airport Express 300 bus operates between the airport and Belfast every 10–20 minutes and leaves from the bus stop opposite the terminal exit. The bus stops at Laganside Buscentre and Europa Buscentre (approximate journey time 30–40 minutes, depending on traffic). There are also approved taxis available outside the terminal.

George Best Belfast City Airport is between Belfast and Holywood, five miles from the city centre. There are two shops

◆ *Airport Express buses connect both airports to the city*

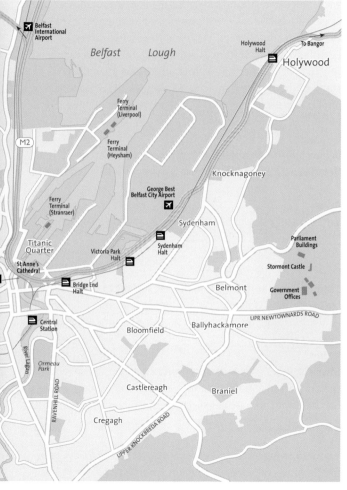

and a range of restaurants/snack bars, as well as cash dispensers, bureaux de change and wireless internet access.

A shuttle bus operates between the airport and the Sydenham railway station. Translink operates a twice-hourly rail service to Belfast Central, Botanic and Great Victoria Street stations (journey time up to 15 minutes). Flexibus operates the Airport Express bus service (route 600) every 20 minutes from the airport terminal to Belfast Europa Bus Centre, which takes 13 minutes.

Belfast International Airport Ⓦ www.belfastairport.com
George Best Belfast City Airport Ⓦ www.belfastcityairport.com

By rail

Belfast railway stations include Belfast Central, Great Victoria Street, Botanic and City Hospital.

By sea

There is a ferry port in Belfast, close to the city centre. The city centre is within walking distance but if you're not up for walking and/or have luggage a cab will cost just a few pounds.

By bus

Long-distance buses arrive at Europa Buscentre, which leads on to Great Victoria Street, next to the Europa Hotel and just a few minutes' walk from Donegall Square and City Hall.

By car

Visitors arriving by car at Belfast ferry port should follow signs for the A2, M3 or Belfast city centre. From Larne ferry port head for the A8, then M2 and A2. From north and northwest you'll arrive via the M2, from the south via the M1 or A1.

FINDING YOUR FEET

Visitors to Belfast will be greeted with a warm Northern Irish welcome and the locals are keen to show that the city has a lot to offer. People are generally easygoing and it won't be difficult to quickly immerse yourself into the *craic* (good time). It isn't a large city, so even if you wander down a side street in the city centre, it won't be long before you find your way back to a main road. If you do get lost, just ask directions – you'll find that people are willing to help.

ORIENTATION

Belfast city centre is bound by the Westlink (which links the M2 and the M1) to the north and west, by the M2 and River Lagan to the east, and Shaftesbury Square to the south. At the heart of the city centre is Donegall Square with the landmark City Hall at its centre. North of Donegall Square are the main shopping streets of Donegall Place, Royal Avenue, High Street and Cornmarket and the oldest parts of the city. The Cathedral Quarter is located at the northern end of the city centre around Donegall Street. Heading east, High Street crosses Victoria Street and leads to the Albert Clock, Custom House Square and the River Lagan. To the south along the river are the Lagan Lookout, the Waterfront Hall and Central Station.

GETTING AROUND

Visitors can easily walk around the city centre on foot, and even

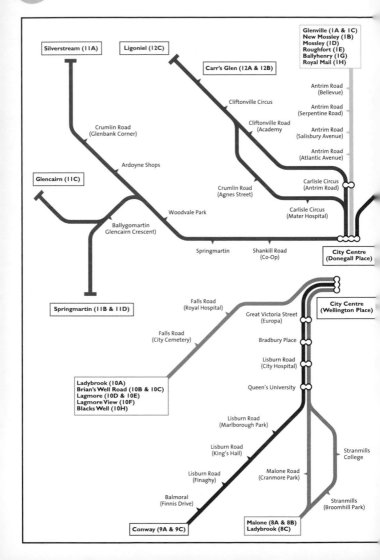

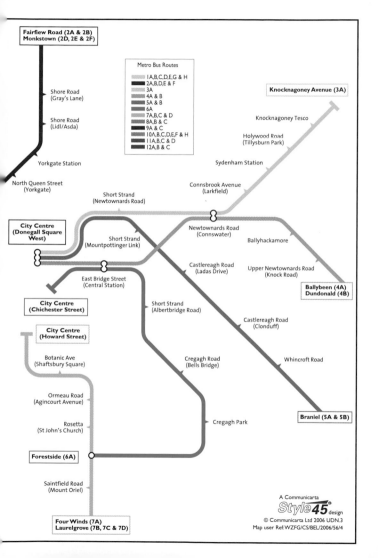

Fairfiew Road (2A & 2B)
Monkstown (2D, 2E & 2F)

Metro Bus Routes
1A,B,C,D,E,G & H
2A,B,D,E & F
3A
4A & B
5A & B
6A
7A,B,C & D
8A,B & C
9A & C
10A,B,C,D,E,F & H
11A,B,C & D
12A,B & C

Knocknagoney Avenue (3A)

Shore Road
(Gray's Lane)

Knocknagoney Tesco

Shore Road
(Lidl/Asda)

Holywood Road
(Tillysburn Park)

Yorkgate Station

Sydenham Station

North Queen Street
(Yorkgate)

Connsbrook Avenue
(Larkfield)

Short Strand
(Newtownards Road)

City Centre
(Donegall Square
West)

Newtownards Road
(Connswater)

Ballyhackamore

Short Strand
(Mountpottinger Link)

Castlereagh Road
(Ladas Drive)

Upper Newtownards Road
(Knock Road)

Ballybeen (4A)
Dundonald (4B)

East Bridge Street
(Central Station)

City Centre
(Chichester Street)

Short Strand
(Albertbridge Road)

Castlereagh Road
(Clonduff)

City Centre
(Howard Street)

Botanic Ave
(Shaftsbury Square)

Whincroft Road

Cregagh Road
(Bells Bridge)

Ormeau Road
(Agincourt Avenue)

Braniel (5A & 5B)

Rosetta
(St John's Church)

Cregagh Park

Forestside (6A)

Saintfield Road
(Mount Oriel)

A Communicarta
Style 45 design
© Communicarta Ltd 2006 UDN.3
Map user Ref:WZFG/CS/BEL/2006/56/4

Four Winds (7A)
Laurelgrove (7B, 7C & 7D)

south to the Ulster Museum, west along Falls and Shankill roads, or along the riverfront. However, for longer distances or if you're tired, there is an efficient urban bus service which is called the Metro, with main departure points in Donegall Square and Wellington Place. You can buy Metro day tickets, giving you the freedom to hop on and off buses as you please. You can buy these from the driver or from the Metro Ticket and Information kiosk in Donegall Square West.

Alternatively, there are shared black taxis that charge a similar rate to buses, operating from Bedford Street (off High Street) to the Shankill Road or from the car park on the corner of Castle Street and King Street. To get further afield, buses from Laganside Buscentre go to North Down, while Europa Buscentre serves the rest of the province, Dublin and international destinations.

CAR HIRE

If you're only planning on staying in Belfast, you don't really need to hire a car. However, if you want the freedom to get around outside the city as you please, then car hire is available at both Belfast International Airport and George Best Belfast City Airport.

Avis ☎ 028 9442 2333 ⓦ www.avis.co.uk
Budget ☎ 028 9442 3332 ⓦ www.budget.ie
Europcar ☎ 028 9442 3444 ⓦ www.europcar.co.uk
Hertz ☎ 028 9442 2533 ⓦ www.hertz.co.uk
National Car Rental ☎ 028 9442 2285 ⓦ www.nationalcar.co.uk

▶ *City Hall*

THE CITY OF
Belfast

City Centre

The oldest part of Belfast is High Street and Castle Place, where the city's first castle once stood. Off here you'll discover various 'entries', side alleys with historic pubs and bars hidden away, and at the end

🔺 *The Albert Memorial Clock*

the iconic Albert Clock. Just north of here is the artsy Cathedral Quarter, around Donegall Street, with St Anne's Cathedral at its centre. Today the heart of the city has shifted south to Donegall Square, where City Hall marks Belfast's city status.

SIGHTS & ATTRACTIONS

Albert Memorial Clock

Built between 1865–70 as a memorial to Queen Victoria's late consort, the Albert Memorial Clock is now one of the city's primary landmarks, partly because of its distinctive lean of around 1.4 m (4.5 ft), blamed on the fact that it was built on reclaimed land. Constructed in 1865 from sandstone, and standing over 34 m (111 ft) high, the clock has a life-size statue of Prince Albert on the west side and a 2-tonne bell.

ⓐ Victoria Street ⓝ Bus: Laganside Buscentre

Belfast Cathedral

Also known as The Cathedral Church of St Anne (or St Anne's Cathedral), this was Belfast's first Church of Ireland parish. The first foundation stone was laid in 1899 but it wasn't completed until 1981.

ⓐ Lower Donegall Street ⓣ 028 9032 8332
ⓦ www.belfastcathedral.org ⓔ vicar@belfastcathedral.org.uk
ⓛ 10.00–16.00 Mon–Sat ⓝ Bus: Royal Avenue

Belfast sightseeing bus tour

The quickest way to get a flavour of the city, buses leave at regular intervals from Castle Place and follow a circular route

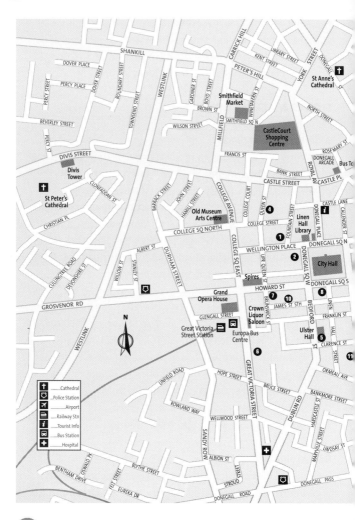

Map legend:

- Cathedral
- Police Station
- Airport
- Railway Stn
- Tourist Info
- Bus Station
- Hospital

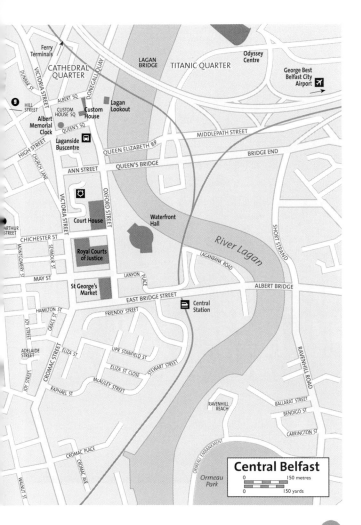

Central Belfast

0 — 150 metres
0 — 150 yards

◔ *Belfast Cathedral*

taking in Belfast city centre, Titanic Quarter, Cathedral Quarter, political murals along the Falls Road and Shankill Road, the Peace Line, University District and the nightlife areas. You're given a route map on the bus and there is a live commentary by a local guide on the way. You can hop on and off *en route*.
ⓐ Castle Place ⓣ 028 9062 6888
ⓦ www.belfastcitysightseeing.com ⓛ 10.00–16.00 daily, tours every 45 minutes (Sept–May), tours every 30 minutes (Jun–Aug) 09.30–16.30 daily ⓝ Bus: Royal Avenue, Donegall Square. Admission charge

Cathedral Quarter

One of the oldest city districts, the Cathedral Quarter had become quite run down, but it's now seeing something of a renaissance. The main focal point is Belfast Cathedral (see above) on Donegall Street and the roads and alleys around it. A favourite with artists and musicians, theatre groups and dance studios due to the low rents, it is fast becoming a trendy arts/media area with new companies moving in and restorations taking place. Look out for the Duke of York pub (see page 74), the original premises of the Northern Bank, Irish News, News Letter and St Patrick's Church, as well as community arts centres and galleries.
ⓐ Donegall Street ⓝ Bus: Royal Avenue

City Hall

Built in Classical Renaissance style and opened in 1906, City Hall stands on the site of the old White Linen Hall. Plans for the building began after Queen Victoria gave Belfast city status in 1888, but construction only began ten years later under the

architect Sir Brumwell Thomas. Highlights include the grand
entrance, main dome with whispering gallery, grand staircase
and the mural by Belfast artist John Luke. The ample grounds
are popular with office workers taking their lunch break in the
sun. The front gates are a popular hangout for Goths, bikers and
anyone else looking for a meeting place, plus there are often
events in front of the building with temporary stages put up
for concerts.

ⓐ Donegall Square ⓣ 028 9032 0202; 028 9027 0405 minicom
ⓕ 028 90315252 ⓦ www.belfastcity.gov.uk ⓛ 09.00–17.00
Mon–Fri; tours 11.00, 14.00 and 15.00 Mon–Fri; 14.00 and 15.00
Sat ⓝ Bus: Donegall Square ⓘ Refurbishment work for City Hall
is planned for some time in 2007 but it hasn't yet been decided
whether they will close or partially close the building when
works are taking place.

Crown Liquor Saloon

A popular venue with locals and tourists, this is a fine example
of a Victorian public house or 'gin palace', now owned by the
National Trust. The outside is clad in colourful tiles, while the
inside is a rich mix of carved wooden snugs, red granite-top bar,
mosaics, tiles, mirrors and columns.

ⓐ 46 Great Victoria Street ⓣ 028 9027 9901
ⓦ www.crownbar.com ⓔ info@crownbar.com ⓝ Bus: Europa
Buscentre, Donegall Square

Custom House Square

Recently renovated to highlight its original use as a speakers'
corner, the paved square now has a bronze statue of 'The

An old Belfast story has it that the name of The Crown Liquor Saloon was chosen by the Protestant wife of the landlord to show her allegiance to the British monarchy. Her husband, a Catholic, wasn't keen on this idea, and only agreed if he could put a mosaic of a crown in the doorway – that way everyone would have to step on it as they walked in to the pub. The mosaic, together with the Crown's celebrated Victorian snugs (complete with antique bells for getting the attention of the bar staff), is still there to greet visitors today.

Speaker' and large copper-based lights along its edge representing 'The Hecklers'. The historic Calder Fountain has also been restored, and lights follow the course of the underground River Farset (which runs the length of High Street). The square is now used for concerts, festivals and other events as well as being a favourite hangout for skateboarders. The central focus of the square is the mid-19th-century **Custom House**, one of the few remaining Custom Houses in the UK still occupied by Her Majesty's Revenue and Customs Officers. It is open to the public on European Heritage Open Days only.

ⓐ Custom House Square ⓝ Bus: Laganside Buscentre

CULTURE

Catalyst Arts

One of the city's fringe arts centres, this artist-run venue supports innovative projects in art, film, photography, music and literature.

ⓐ 2nd Floor, 5 College Court ① 028 9031 3303
ⓦ www.catalystarts.org.uk ⓔ info@catalystarts.org.uk
⏱ Various ⓝ Bus: Donegall Square/Royal Avenue.
Admission charge

Grand Opera House

You're unlikely to see opera at this historic venue but you can catch off-West End theatre, musicals and pantomimes. The renovated opera house now has an extension that has added an all-day café/bistro, bars and more wheelchair space and access.
ⓐ Great Victoria Street ① 028 9024 1919 ⓦ www.goh.co.uk
⏱ Various ⓝ Bus: Europa Buscentre/Donegall Square

Linen Hall Library

Founded in 1788, the Linen Hall contains the best Irish and Local Studies Collection of books covering everything from early Belfast and Ulster to the contemporary NI Political Collection on The Troubles. A centre of cultural and creative life, it hosts a varied programme of exhibitions, readings, discussion groups and lectures. Use the library for reference or read a few of your favourite newspapers.
ⓐ 17 Donegall Square North ① 028 9032 1707 ① 028 9043 8586
ⓦ www.linenhall.com ⓔ info@linenhall.com ⏱ 09.30–17.30
Mon–Fri, 09.30–13.00 Sat ⓝ Bus: Donegall Square

Old Museum Arts Centre

Presents contemporary theatre, music, dance and visual art from Northern Ireland and overseas. Plans are underway to build a state-of-the-art replacement in the Cathedral Quarter.

ⓐ 7 College Square North ⓣ 028 9023 5053
ⓦ www.oldmuseumartscentre.org ⓛ various ⓝ Donegall
Square. Admission charge

Ulster Hall

You can see theatre, classical concerts and jazz here.
ⓐ Bedford Street ⓣ 028 9032 3900 ⓦ www.ulsterhall.co.uk
ⓔ ulsterhall@belfastcity.gov.uk ⓛ Various ⓝ Bus: Donegall Square

Waterfront Hall

Opened in 1997 as the flagship building for the Laganside
development, the Waterfront Hall is the city's major concert and
conference venue, hosting opera, classical and popular concerts.
ⓐ Lanyon Place ⓣ 028 9033 4455 ⓦ www.waterfront.co.uk
ⓛ various ⓝ Bus: Laganside Bus Station. Admission charge

RETAIL THERAPY

Main shopping areas

The hub of Belfast's shopping is around **Donegall Place** and
Royal Avenue, where you'll find high-street stores, Marks and
Spencer and the large **CastleCourt shopping centre**,
ⓦ www.westfield.com/castlecourt, with two floors of shops and
eateries. **Royal Arcade** (off Royal Avenue) has jewellery and gift
shops. More shops can be found along **High Street** and
Cornmarket. Inside **Donegall Arcade** (Castle Place) look out for
the **WickerMan**, ⓦ www.thewickerman.co.uk, which sells Celtic
crafts and souvenirs. The **Spires Centre** is another small

shopping centre, converted from a former Presbyterian Church House and Assembly Hall.

Markets

St George's Market on Oxford Street is a late 19th-century market that's had a makeover, buffing up its Victorian splendour. On Friday there's a vibrant mixed market (06.00–13.00) and on Saturday jazz and food at the City Food &

🔺 *Hit St George's Market at dawn on Friday*

Garden Market (10.00–16.00). Catch the free market bus on market days from Donegall Place or Castle Place. **Smithfield Market,** in West Street/Winetavern Street opposite CastleCourt, sells a little of everything, from leather and picture frames to second-hand goods, Mon–Sat (09.00–17.00).

TAKING A BREAK

Altos Café Bar Restaurant £ ❶ Family-run café opposite City Hall selling healthy lunches, burgers, veggie options, coffee, scones, and beer. You can also eat outside. ⓐ Unit 6, Fountain Street ☎ 028 9032 3087 🕑 10.00–17.00 Mon–Wed 10.00–20.00 Thur, 10.00–18.00 Fri & Sat

Apartment £ ❷ Trendy restaurant-bar serving paninis and modern European food with downstairs booths and upstairs tables and sofa dining plus views of City Hall. ⓐ 2 Donegall Square West ☎ 028 9050 9777 ⓦ www.apartmentbelfast.com ⓔ info@apartmentbelfast.com 🕑 Mon–Fri 08.00–01.00 (last food orders 21.00), Sat 09.00–01.00, Sun 12.00–01.00

Café Paul Rankin £ ❸ Owned by TV chef Paul Rankin, this café serves deli sandwiches, soups and salads. There's also a branch in CastleCourt shopping centre. ⓐ 12–14 Arthur Street ☎ 028 9031 0108 ⓦ www.rankingroup.co.uk 🕑 07.30–17.30 Mon–Wed & Thur–Sat, 07.30–19.00 (Thur), 13.00–17.00 Sun

Café Renoir £ ❹ Try homemade scones, fresh bread and organic jams from the Loney family farm. The triple club sandwich is particularly popular. ⓐ 5–7 Queen Street ❶ 028 9032 5592 ⓦ www.cafe-renoir.com 🕐 09.00–17.00 Mon–Sat, except 09.00–19.30 Thur

Deanes Deli £ ❺ Michelin-star chef Michael Deane's New York-style deli with olives, charcuterie boards, burgers, salads and soup for lunch and steaks and fish and chips in the evening. The adjacent store sells Deane's branded products. ⓐ 44 Bedford Street ❶ 028 9024 8800 ⓦ www.michaeldeane.co.uk ⓔ info@michaeldeane.co.uk 🕐 11.30–21.00 Mon & Tues, 11.30–22.00 Wed–Sat, closed Sun

AFTER DARK

Restaurants
The Red Panda £ ❻ Renowned Chinese restaurant in the Golden Mile. ⓐ 60 Great Victoria Street ❶ 028 9080 8700 ⓦ www.theredpanda.co.uk 🕐 12.00–14.30 Mon–Fri, 12.30–15.30 Sun (lunch); 17.00–late Mon–Sat, 15.30–late Sun (dinner)

Deanes Brasserie ££ ❼ Sophisticated brasserie where you can treat yourself to Irish dishes such as local smoked salmon and steak & Guinness pie. ⓐ 34–40 Howard Street ❶ 028 9056 0000 ❶ 028 9056 0001 ⓦ www.michaeldeane.co.uk ⓔ info@michaeldeane.co.uk 🕐 12.00–15.00 Mon–Sat (lunch); 17.30–22.00 Mon–Thur, 17.30–23.00 Fri–Sat (dinner); closed Sun

The Grill Room & Bar ££ ❽ Stop for a cocktail or two and hear the in-house band every Wed and Sun. ⓐ Ten Square Hotel,

10 Donegall Square ⓣ 028 9024 1001 ⓦ www.tensquare.co.uk
ⓛ 07.30–01.00 Mon–Sat, 08.00–24.00 Sun; food served
till 10pm

Hill Street Brasserie ££ ⓽ Cathedral Quarter restaurant
serving modern Mediterranean dishes using fresh ingredients;
one of the first to ban smoking. ⓐ 38 Hill Street ⓣ 028 9058
6868 ⓦ www.hillstbrasserie.com ⓛ 12.00–15.00 Mon–Sat,
17.00–23.00 Tues–Sat

James Street South ££ ⓾ European cuisine in contemporary
surroundings with set lunch and pre-theatre menus. ⓐ 21 James
Street South ⓣ 028 9043 4310 ⓦ www.jamesstreetsouth.co.uk
ⓛ 12.00–14.45 & 17.45–22.45 Mon–Sat, 17.30–21.00 Sun

Zen Restaurant £££ ⓫ Excellent Japanese restaurant serving
fusion food. ⓐ 55–59 Adelaide Street ⓣ 028 9023 2244
ⓛ 12.00–15.00 & 17.00–23.30 Mon–Fri, 18.00–01.00 Sat,
13.30–22.00 Sun

Bars/clubs
Café Vaudeville A former bank that's had an extravagant
makeover turning it into the glitziest venue in the city, with high
ceilings, chandeliers and gilt-frame pictures giving it a
yesteryear feel. Stop for coffee, tea, modern European food,
beers and cocktails, or pre-book for the 'Bolly bar' upstairs.
ⓐ 25–39 Arthur Street ⓣ 028 9043 9160
ⓦ www.cafevaudeville.com ⓔ info@cafevaudeville.com
ⓛ 11.30–01.00 Mon–Sat, 12.00–00.00 Sun

Crown Liquor Saloon A pint in this historic Belfast pub is a must. Sit in a snug or at the bar with a pint or lunch in the Crown Dining Rooms upstairs, which features local specialities like sausage and champ. ⓐ 46 Great Victoria Street ⓣ 028 9027 9901 ⓦ www.crownbar.com ⓔ info@crownbar.com

Duke of York One of the oldest pubs in the city, in its heyday it was frequented by the literati, politicians and hacks who worked in the nearby newspaper industry. Sit in a snug and enjoy a few pints and traditional Irish food. ⓐ Commercial Court, Cathedral Quarter ⓣ 028 9024 1062 ⓛ 11.30–01.00 daily

The John Hewitt Traditional bar with live music three nights a week; popular with local artists, writers and journalists. ⓐ 51 Donegall Street ⓣ 028 9023 3768 ⓦ www.thejohnhewitt.com ⓛ 11.30–01.00 Mon–Fri, 12.00–01.00 Sat, doesn't always open on Sun

The Kitchen Bar This famous old bar was once the haunt of visiting stars of the stage but has recently been moved down the street to make way for the new Victoria Square retail development. Now housed in a renovated Victorian warehouse, there's food, live music in the bar and sports on the plasma screens. ⓐ 36–40 Victoria Square ⓣ 028 9032 4901 ⓛ 11.30–01.00 Mon–Wed, 11.30–00.00 Thur, 11.30–01.00 Fri & Sat, 11.00–18.00 Sun

The Limelight / Spring & Airbrake / Katy Daly's Three venues in one, Katy Daly's is a good place for cheap eats. The Limelight is

Belfast's best live music venue, closely followed by Spring & Airbreak. They also host club nights from 60s to Skool Disco.
ⓐ 15–17 Ormeau Avenue ⓣ 028 9032 5968
ⓦ www.the-limelight.co.uk ⓛ varies

Kremlin Gay bar decorated to recall Soviet Russia, it hosts themed nights such as fetish nights, transvestite shows and foam parties.
ⓐ 96 Donegall Street ⓣ 028 9031 6067
ⓦ www.kremlin-belfast.com ⓛ 21.00–02.30 Tues, 21.00–03.00 Thur–Sun

Mynt Formerly Parliament, this was Belfast's first gay bar and is still its biggest with a lounge bar and two club rooms with more in the pipeline. You can eat international food here, stop for a drink or stay for the late-night entertainment. ⓐ 2–16 Dunbar Street ⓣ 028 9023 4520 ⓦ www.myntbelfast.com ⓛ 12.00–15.00 Mon–Fri, 12.00–16.00 Sat, 13.00–16.00 Sun (lunch); 23.00–very late Fri–Sun (club)

Robinson's Bars Four venues under one roof, including the saloon bar **Fibber McGee's** in the back with live traditional music, BT1 basement chill-out bar and Mezza(nine) club.
ⓐ 38–42 Great Victoria Street ⓣ 028 9024 7447 ⓛ 11.30–01.00 Mon–Sat, 12.30–00.00 Sun

White's Tavern Claims to be the oldest pub in Belfast, just off High Street. Home-made food is served during the day and there are live bands on Fridays and Saturdays. ⓐ 2–4 Winecellar Entry ⓣ 028 9024 3080 ⓛ 11.30–23.00 Mon–Sat

North & West Belfast

The Falls and Shankill roads are among the most notorious in
Belfast, a hotspot for nationalist and loyalist clashes during The
Troubles, but these areas had been divided along religious lines
way before the recent conflict. When migrants poured into
Belfast during the Industrial Revolution they flocked to areas
that were already either Catholic or Protestant, bringing their
rivalries with them. The Shankill Road, which stands between
West Belfast and North Belfast, was actually the sight of
settlements dating back to the Stone Age, but its name derives
from the Gaelic *Sean Cill*, meaning 'old church'. Today there's
nothing Gaelic about the Shankill and despite the official end of
the armed struggle, it remains run down, struggling to rebuild
its community, displaying its identity through murals and flags.
Tourists are attracted here to see the murals and the peace line
that divides it from the Catholic Falls Road. A symbol of
Republican West Belfast, the Falls Road was extremely deprived,
maybe even more so in the 1960s, but today it is celebrating its
Irishness with Irish names, Celtic script on signs and Irish
cultural centres and sports. You should visit the murals in both
areas to begin to understand the origins and impact of the
conflict. In general most visitors prefer to eat, drink and stay in
the city centre or South Belfast, but the locals are encouraging
tourism by opening their own B&Bs. Overlooking West Belfast,
the hills of Cave Hill Country Park are a must-see, with Belfast
Castle, its Visitor Centre and trails to McArt's Fort providing an
insight into the city's history. Nearby Belfast Zoo provides light
relief for children.

SIGHTS & ATTRACTIONS

Belfast Castle

The original Belfast Castle was built by the Normans in the 12th century in what is now the city centre (Castle Street). Another castle followed on the same site, but this was burned down in the early 18th century, and it was the Marquis of Donegall who commissioned the current building on the slopes of Cave Hill. It was finished in 1870 and presented to the City of Belfast in 1934. It has been a popular location for weddings, dances and afternoon teas ever since. You can visit the castle but access depends on what events are taking place. There is also a shop and restaurant, as well as a Visitor Centre on the second floor

◔ *Cave Hill Country Park overlooks the city*

North & West Belfast

| 0 | 600 metres |
| 0 | 600 yards |

CATHEDRAL
........Cathedral
........Police Station
........Airport
......Railway Stn
........Bus Station
........Hospital

BALLYSILLAN
LIGONIEL
FORTWILLIAM
Cave Hill Coutry Park
Belfast Castle & Belfast Zoo
Cliftonville Golf Course
CRUMLIN ROAD
NORTH CIRCULAR ROAD
LIGONIEL ROAD
BALLYSILLAN PARK
SUNNINGDALE PARK
CAVEHILL AVENUE
SALISBURY AVENUE
ANTRIM ROAD
SILVERSTREAM RD
BALLYSILLAN ROAD
OLDPARK ROAD
OLDPARK TER
WESTLAND ROAD
DEERPARK ROAD
OLDPARK
ALLIANCE ROAD
BENVICK ST
CLIFTONVILLE ROAD
ANTRIM RD
CLIFTONVILLE
ARDOYNE
CRUMLIN ROAD
Fernhill House
GLENCAIRN
Glencairn Park
FORTHRIVER ROAD
GLENCAIRN ROAD
BROMPTON PK
OLDPARK ROAD
CLIFTONPARK AVE
CAMBRAI ST
TENNENT STREET
SHANKILL
CRUMLIN ROAD
AGNES ST
Orange Hall
WEST CIRCULAR ROAD
BALLYGOMARTIN ROAD
SPRINGMARTIN
SHANKILL ROAD
SPRINGMARTIN RD
SPRINGFIELD RD
CONARD GDNS
DIVIS ST
St Peter's Cathedral
Divis Tower
FALLS
Garden of Remembrance
GROSVENOR ROAD
Great Victoria Street Station
BALLYMURPHY
Culturlann MacAdam
FALLS ROAD
SPRINGFIELD ROAD
WESTLINK
RODEN ST
Colin Glen Forest Park
WHITEROCK ROAD
FALLSWATER STREET
DONEGALL ROAD
DONEGALL
City Hospital Halt
TURF LODGE
Belfast City Cemetery
M1
DUNLUCE AVE
LISBURN ROAD
Milltown Cemetery
Windsor Park Football Ground
TATE'S AVENUE

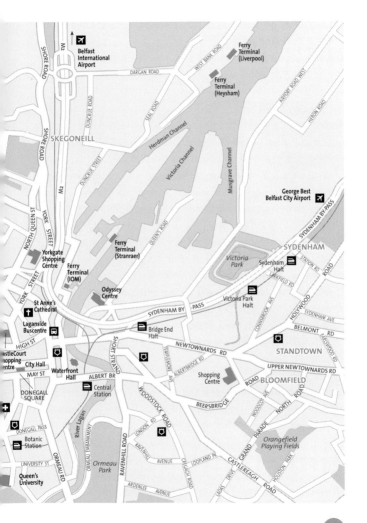

with exhibits on both the history of the castle and Cave Hill
Country Park (see page 82).

ⓐ Antrim Road ⓣ 028 9077 6925 ⓦ www.belfastcastle.co.uk
ⓛ 09.00–22.00 Mon–Sat, 09.00–18.00 Sun ⓝ Bus: 1A–D

Belfast City Cemetery

Belfast City Cemetery is a mixed cemetery located in a
nationalist area. Before it opened in 1869, a wall was built
underground to symbolically divide the Catholic and Protestant
areas. Look out for the graves of some famous Belfast residents,
including the writer Robert Wilson Lynd, Viscount Pirrie
(chairman of Harland and Wolff during the building of the
Titanic), Sir Edward Harland (one of the founders of Harland
Wolff) and Denis Donaldson, former IRA member and Sinn Féin
official, who was killed in 2006 after it was announced that he
had been a spy for the British Government. Tours are available.
ⓐ Falls Road ⓣ 028 9032 0202 ⓛ 08.00–18.00 Mon–Sat,
10.00–18.00 Sun (Mar & Oct); 08.00–18.00 Mon, Wed, Fri & Sat,
08.00–20.00 Tues & Thur, 10.00–18.00 Sun (Apr–Sept);
08.00–16.00 Mon–Sat, 10.00–16.00 Sun (Nov–Feb) ⓝ Bus: 10A–F

Belfast Zoo

Located in North Belfast near the Castle (see page 77), the zoo
aims to help endangered species of animals from around the
world. Divided into continental areas, you can see Rothschild's
giraffe, gorilla and the white-crested turaco in Africa, leaf
monkey, tiger and elephant in Asia, and the Andean bear, spider
monkey and vincuña in South America, among others. You can
also eat at The Ark Restaurant or The Mountain Teahouse.

ⓐ Antrim Road ⓣ 028 9077 6277 ⓦ www.belfastzoo.co.uk
ⓛ 10.00–17.00 last admission (Apr–Sept); 10.00–14.30 last
admission (Oct–Mar) ⓝ 10A-F, 2A. Admission charge

Black Cab Tours NI

A good alternative to other official tours, the Black Cab Tours
offer an insiders' view of the city. Belfast tours take in the
Shankill and Falls Road murals, Milltown Cemetery, Stormont,
Queen's University, City Hall and Belfast Castle. It is more
expensive, but you can stop to take pictures or buy souvenirs

🔺 *Black cab tours take in the famous murals*

and can ask questions as you go. You can also hire cabs to go on a Causeway Coast tour or devise your own itinerary.

t 07754 095736 **w** www.blackcabtoursni.com
e blackcabtoursni@hotmail.com **l** by arrangement **n** Pick up at your hotel

Cave Hill Country Park

Rising up 368 m (1,207 ft) behind the city, Cave Hill is one of the city's most celebrated landmarks and the location of Belfast Castle (see page 77). Since 1992 it has been a Country Park and wildlife refuge for a variety of animals and birds, as well as containing two nature reserves, Ballyhagan and Hazelwood. One of the most noticeable features of the park is Napoleon's Nose, an outcrop on the top of the hill, which can be seen from the city centre. Also known as McArt's Fort, It was here that the leaders of the 1798 rebellion took an oath to fight for Ireland's liberation from English rule. You can discover more about the history of the area at the Visitor Centre inside the Castle and also explore the park via way-marked paths

a Antrim Road **l** Dawn till dusk **n** Bus: 1A-F

Coiste Political Tours

Another way to see the city is to take a tour round republican and loyalist areas with the ex-prisoner community. Starting from Divis Tower at Westlink end of the Falls Road, you get to hear some very different viewpoints on the conflict. The walking tours last around two hours, but booking is essential – you can even organise tours in Spanish, Basque, Irish or French.

a Divis Tower, Falls Road **t** 020 9020 0070

ⓦ www.coiste.ie/politicaltours ⓔ caoimhin@coiste.com
ⓛ Walking tour 11.00 Mon–Sat; 14.00 Sun ⓝ Walk or take
collective black taxi from Castle Street car park.
Admission charge

Divis Tower

Divis Tower might seem like any ordinary tower block, but from
the 1970s the top two floors were occupied by the British army as
a lookout point over Divis flats around the tower (which were
demolished in the early 1980s), up the Falls Road and towards the
city centre. The troops finally moved out in 2005, but the tower is
still an iconic building in the history of The Troubles.
ⓐ Divis Street ⓝ Walk from city centre or take black taxi from
Castle Street car park.

Fernhill House – The People's Museum

The museum outlines the social, economic and military history of
the Greater Shankill area. It is located in Fernhill House, a 19th-
century house which became a museum in 1996 to promote
understanding of the area. Exhibits cover themes of working,
living in a small house, the Red Cross, football and World War II.
ⓐ Glencairn Park ⓣ 028 9071 5599 ⓦ www.fernhillhouse.co.uk
ⓛ 10.00–16.00 Mon–Sat, 13.00–16.00 Sun ⓝ Bus: 11C.
Admission charge

Garden of Remembrance

Walking up the Falls Road, just before you arrive at the library
and Sinn Féin bookshop on the right-hand side, you'll see a small
garden on the left. This is one of many memorials to those who

died in The Troubles. Being in the Falls Road, this is dedicated to republicans (including the hunger striker Bobby Sands), with the Irish tricolour flying above.

🅐 Falls Road 🔃 Walk from city centre or take a black taxi from Castle Street car park

Milltown Cemetery

Located along the Falls Road, this is a Catholic cemetery where you'll find IRA and other republican memorials. A sea of Celtic crosses, the cemetery has a backdrop of the Belfast hills and views across the M1 motorway towards the city centre. Look out for the green field of unmarked paupers' graves, where victims of cholera, typhoid and flu were buried.

🅐 Falls Road 🔃 Bus: 10A-F. Walk from city centre or take black taxi from Castle Street car park

> ### MILLTOWN: REFLECTING BELFAST'S TROUBLED PAST
> In 1988, the loyalist paramilitary Michael Stone killed two mourners and a Provisional IRA member, and injured around 50 more people at a funeral at Milltown Cemetery for the Gibraltar Three (three IRA members killed by the SAS in Gibraltar). The cemetery also contains the graves of Bobby Sands and the other hunger strikers who died in 1981. Look at the plots more carefully and you'll notice that the republican plots are divided up into Official IRA, Provisional IRA, INLA and Real IRA.

⬥ *A sea of Celtic crosses: Milltown Cemetery*

Orange Hall

As you cross the Westlink towards Crumlin Road, you will see an Orange Hall on the left-hand side. On the top is a statue of 'King Billy', William of Orange, who defeated King James I in the famous Battle of the Boyne in 1690. Today this is a renowned starting point for Orange Order marches.

ⓐ Carlisle Circus Ⓝ Bus: 1A, 1B, 1E

Peace Line

This is a steel wall that divides the nationalist Falls Road area from the loyalist Shankill Road. The best way to see it is on the sightseeing bus tour.

ⓐ West Belfast Ⓝ Bus: 10A-F

St Peter's Cathedral

Belfast's Roman Catholic cathedral was built in the 19th century to cope with the large numbers of workers who had come to work in the linen mills nearby. Its position made it a prominent landmark with five doorways, two porch entrances and a sculpture depicting the liberation of St Peter from prison over the main entrance, plus its iconic twin spires, which were added a few years later.

ⓐ Derby Street ☎ 028 9032 7573 🖶 028 9032 5570
ⓦ www.stpeterscathedralbelfast.com

West Belfast murals

The political murals in West Belfast have become one of the city's most popular tourist attractions. You can get a quick overview on a bus tour but to get a closer look you either need to take a private black cab tour (see page 81) or go on foot. There are some interesting murals in East Belfast too but they are not as accessible as those along the nationalist Falls Road and the loyalist Shankill Road. You'll see murals on the side of virtually every corner building along the streets. In the Falls Road these range from murals showing sympathy for other nationalist and liberation movements, such as those in Palestine and Catalonia and images depicting the 1916 Easter Rising, hunger strikers and other 'fallen' IRA comrades. Along the Shankill Road you can see images of the Derry Apprentice Boys slamming the gates of the city in 1688 and the Battle of the Boyne in 1690, as well as murals supporting loyalist paramilitary groups such as the Ulster Volunteer Force (UVF) and Ulster Defence Association (UDA). ⓐ Falls and Shankill roads Ⓝ Sightseeing bus tour, black taxi tour or on foot

CULTURE

Cultúrlann MacAdam

The centre of the Falls Road Gaeltacht (Irish-speaking) community, it runs Irish language courses, has a bookshop and tourist point (with help on accommodation), and hosts art, music, drama and literature events. Hear some live traditional Irish music in the café/restaurant every week – they welcome passing musicians too! Buy an Irish language course in the shop, hear locals chatting in Irish in the café or stay for one of the other events. ⓐ 216 Falls Road ⓣ 028 9096 4180 ⓦ www.culturlann.com ⓔ oifigfailte@culturlann.ie Ⓛ 09.00–17.30 Mon–Fri, 10.00–17.00 Sat (bookshop); 14.00–20.00 café Ⓝ Any bus from Queen Street in the city centre

RETAIL THERAPY

At Cultúrlann, there's a selection of Irish language and literature books as well as cards and photographs. In Andersonstown there's a large O'Neills International Sportswear shop selling Gaelic football strip, hurley sticks and balls, Ireland rugby tops and Celtic football tops.

TAKING A BREAK

Cultúrlann Café £ ❶ You can stop here for a late lunch, afternoon refreshments or dinner at a reasonable price, while listening to locals chatting in Irish (see page 87). The menu includes fish and chips, lasagne, burgers, wraps and pizzas.
ⓐ 216 Falls Road ⓣ 028 9096 4180 ⓦ www.culturlann.com

The Mountain Teahouse £ ❷ Stop for a coffee, cake and biscuits or other snacks during a visit to Belfast Zoo. ⓐ Belfast Zoo, Antrim Road ⓣ 028 9077 6925 ⓦ www.belfastzoo.co.uk
ⓛ 10.30–17.00 Apr–Sept, closed Oct–Mar

AFTER DARK

Restaurants
The Ark Restaurant £ ❸ Located in Belfast Zoo, this is a good option for the family with hot and cold food and veggie options.
ⓐ Belfast Zoo ⓣ 028 9077 6925 ⓦ www.belfastzoo.co.uk
ⓛ 10.30–17.30 Apr–Sept, 10.30–15.30 Oct–Mar

Cellar Restaurant ££ ❹ This is Belfast Castle's restaurant and serves quality home-grown food in a beautiful historic location. ⓐ Belfast Castle, off Antrim Road ⓣ 028 9077 6925 ⓦ www.belfastcastle.co.uk ⓛ 11.00–17.00 (snacks/light refreshments) Mon–Sat, 12.30–15.00 (lunch) Mon–Sat, 17.00–18.30 (early evening meal), 19.00–21.00 (dinner) Tues–Sat

Pubs

The Beehive A lively local pub with pub grub from fish and chips to curry, plus folk sessions on a Sunday. ⓐ 193 Falls Road ⓣ 028 9032 8439 ⓦ www.whitefortinns.com ⓛ 11.30–23.00 Mon–Sat, 12.00–22.30 Sun

McEnaney's Located opposite Milltown Cemetery, stop at this traditional pub for a pint or two after a long walk from the city centre and if you're lucky you might hear some live traditional music. ⓐ Glen Road, Andersonstown ⓣ 028 9061 ⓛ 11.30–23.00 Mon–Sat, 12.00–22.30 Sun

P & F Gil Martin Traditional Victorian pub with original décor and tiled floor, this is what was traditionally considered as a 'man's pub', where men would bring their wives at weekends only (they drank upstairs). ⓐ Lower Springfield Road ⓛ 11.30–23.00 Mon–Sat, 12.00–22.30 Sun

South & East Belfast

South and East Belfast are adjacent but contrasting areas of Belfast. As the location of Queen's University, the South is considered to be the intellectual centre, but its large student population also gives it a bohemian feel. Cheap student terraced accommodation backs on to leafy avenues of expensive houses; boutique hotels and designer clothes shops along the Lisburn Road lead into wild nights in Bradbury Place and Botanic Avenue. You can walk to Botanic easily from the city centre and even down to Queen's University if you have the feet for it. Beyond that and you'll have to think about taking a bus. Make time to see East Belfast, primarily a residential area but also the location of some key attractions and the gateway to North Down. Take a tour round the Titanic Quarter, the target of a huge makeover that will transform the area and bring work, play, arts, cafés and hotels.

SIGHTS & ATTRACTIONS

Belfast Titanic Trail

This new interactive trail is a self-guided tour using a hand-held media player. It takes you on a multi-media tour of the key city sights associated with the RMS *Titanic*, from City Hall to Queen's Island. It is available for hire from the Belfast Welcome Centre. ⓐ Belfast Welcome Centre, 47 Donegall Place ⓣ 028 9024 6609 ⓦ www.gotobelfast.com ⓛ 09.00–17.00 Mon–Sat (Oct–May); 09.00–19.00 Mon–Sat, 12.00–17.00 Sun (Jun–Sept) ⓝ Bus: Donegall Square. Admission charge

Botanic Gardens Park

Highlights of the park are the restored Victorian Palm House, with a valuable collection of tropical and temperate palms, and Tropical Ravine, with a humid jungle glen and a fish pond filled with giant water lilies. Today it is popular with both locals and visitors for walking, relaxing and taking in the sights and sounds, including occasional events from pop and classical concerts to the annual Garden Gourmet in September.

🅐 Stranmillis Road/Botanic Avenue 🕐 Dawn till dusk 🅝 Bus: 8 to Queens University or 7 to College Park

Lagan Valley Regional Park

This park was established in 1967 and extends more than 10 miles from Stranmillis in South Belfast to Lisburn's Union Locks.

🔺 *The Palm House at Botanic Gardens*

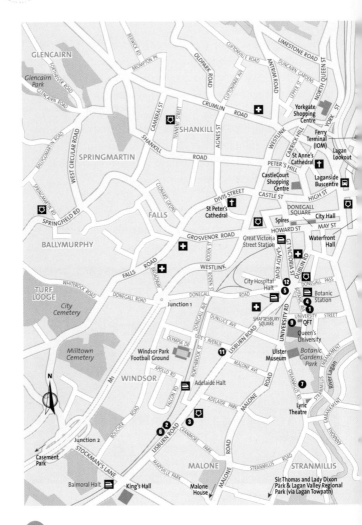

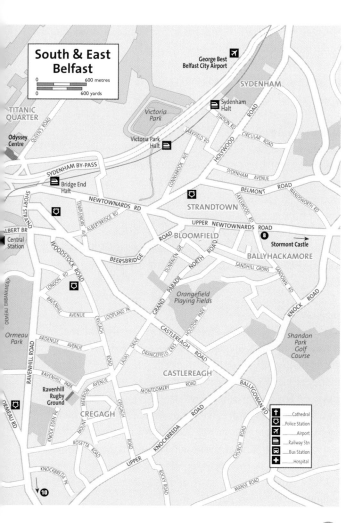

South & East Belfast

0 — 600 metres
0 — 600 yards

George Best
Belfast City Airport

SYDENHAM

TITANIC QUARTER

Victoria Park

Sydenham Halt

STATION RD

HOLYWOOD ROAD

CIRCULAR ROAD

Odyssey Centre

QUEENS ROAD

Victoria Park Halt

YARKFIELD RD

CONNSBROOK AVE

SYDENHAM BY-PASS

SYDENHAM AVENUE

BELMONT ROAD

WANDSWORTH RD

Bridge End Halt

TEMPLEMORE AVE

NEWTOWNARDS RD

ALBERTBRIDGE RD

PARKWOOD

STRANDTOWN

SHORT STRAND

ALBERT BR

Central Station

ALBERTBRIDGE RD

UPPER NEWTOWNARDS ROAD

BLOOMFIELD

ROAD

8

Stormont Castle →

BALLYHACKAMORE

SANDHILL GRDNS

SANDOWN RD

WOODSTOCK ROAD

BEERSBRIDGE

DUNRAVEN AVE

NORTH PARADE

ROAD

KNOCK ROAD

LONDON RD

RAVENHILL

AVENUE

LOOPLAND PK

GRAND PARADE

HOUSTON PARK

Orangefield Playing Fields

ORMEAU EMBANKMENT

Ormeau Park

ARDENLEE

AVENUE

CREGAGH ROAD

LADAS DRIVE

ORANGEFIELD CRES

CASTLEREAGH ROAD

Shandon Park Golf Course

RAVENHILL ROAD

RAVENHILL PARK

MERVIEW AVENUE

CASTLEREAGH ROAD

BALLYGOWAN RD

Ravenhill Rugby Ground

MONTGOMERY ROAD

ORMEAU RD

CREGAGH

MOUNT

CREGAGH ROAD

KNOCKBREDA

ROAD

CHURCH ROAD

KNOCK EDEN PK

ROSETTA ROAD

UPPER KNOCKBREDA

ROCKY ROAD

KNOCKBREDA PK

10

MANSE ROAD

Legend

✝	.....Cathedral
◎	.Police Station
✈	.........Airport
🚆	....Railway Stn
🚌	...Bus Station
✚	.........Hospital

The reach of the park means it is a mosaic of countryside, urban parks, heritage sites, nature reserves and riverside trails and a great break from the city.

ⓐ Lockview Road to Lisburn Union Locks ⓣ 028 9049 1922
ⓦ www.laganvalley.co.uk ⓝ Bus: 8B-C, 8A

Malone House

Malone House is an elegant late Georgian manor located in the South Belfast parkland known as the Barnett Demesne, itself part of the Lagan Valley Regional Park. You can walk through woodland, meadows and marsh. Look out for rabbits, foxes, mink, otters, bats and long-eared owls.

ⓐ Barnett Demesne, Malone Road ⓣ 028 9068 1246
ⓦ www.malonehouse.co.uk ⓒ Park dawn till dusk Mon–Sat;
Malone House 09.00–17.00 Mon–Sat, 11.00–17.00 Sun
ⓝ Bus: 9A-C

Odyssey

A Landmark Millennium Project for Northern Ireland, the Odyssey complex is divided into three main parts:
W5, ⓦ www.w5online.co.uk, is an interactive discovery centre with four dynamic exhibition areas, Start, Go, See and Do, plus changing temporary exhibitions. Here kids (and adults) make a voyage of discovery. You can find out what it's like to be a car mechanic, explore your senses with the sounds and feel of nature in a woodland area, beat the lie detector and bring robots to life.
Odyssey Arena, ⓦ www.odysseyarena.com, is home to the Belfast Giants ice hockey team and also hosts touring shows, exhibitions and concerts.

Odyssey Pavilion, Ⓦ www.odysseypavilion.com, where you'll find an **IMAX cinema**, ten-pin bowling, bars, restaurants and a nightclub, plus a large car park.

ⓐ Queen's Quay Ⓣ 028 9045 1055 Ⓕ 028 9045 1052
Ⓦ www.theodyssey.co.uk Ⓔ info@theodyssey.co.uk Ⓛ Various
Ⓝ Bus: Laganside or shuttle bus during major events from various city centre pick-up points. Admission charge

Ormeau Park

Once part of the demesne of the Donegall family, the estate was sold to the Belfast Corporation in the late 19th century, becoming the first public park in Belfast. It remains one of the largest in the city with woodland, wildlife and nature trails, and hosts various events throughout the year.

ⓐ Ormeau Road Ⓛ Dawn till dusk Ⓝ Bus: 7A, 7D

Queen's University

Founded by Queen Victoria, Queen's University opened in 1840 in the magnificent Lanyon Building, still the most recognisable part of the university. Since then the university estate has grown to include more than 300 buildings. There is a visitor centre inside the Lanyon Building, with a gift shop and exhibitions.

ⓐ University Road Ⓣ 028 9097 5252 Ⓦ www.qub.ac.uk
Ⓔ visitors.centre@qub.ac.uk Ⓛ Visitor Centre 10.00–16.00
Mon–Fri, 10.00–16.00 Sat (May–Sept) Ⓝ Bus: 8A-C

Stormont Castle

The administrative quarters of the Secretary of State for Northern Ireland, this Neoclassical building is located at the end of Prince of Wales Avenue. George Best's funeral was held here in 2005. Unfortunately visitors can't go inside but can walk along the avenue and in the grounds.

ⓐ Upper Newtownards Road ⓦ www.niassembly. gov.uk ⓝ Bus: 23 to Stormont Massey Avenue Gates

Titanic Boat Tours

If you'd rather take to the water than hop on a bus, this is a good way to learn about the history of the *Titanic*. You'll see the offices where the ship was designed, the dry dock where it was worked on and the slipways where it first took to water.

ⓐ Landing Stage, The Lagan Lookout ⓣ 028 9033 0844

🔺 *The imposing approach to Stormont Castle*

Ⓦ www.laganboatcompany.com Ⓛ Five daily departures 11.00, 12.30, 14.00, 15.30, 17.30 Ⓝ Bus: Laganside. Admission charge

BUILDING THE *TITANIC*

By the time Edward Harland died in 1895, the company had become the world's greatest shipbuilders. Designed by Alexander Carlisle and then Thomas Andrews, the floating palace that was the *Titanic* was launched on 31 May 1911 in front of thousands of onlookers. It was taken to Southampton and set off on its maiden voyage from there on 10 April 1912. Four days later, having travelled 1,500 miles, the ship struck an iceberg and was fatally damaged. Of the 2,228 passengers and crew, only 705 survived.

Titanic Quarter

Once the centre of Belfast's great shipbuilding industry, today the former shipyards on Queen's Island are referred to as the Titanic Quarter, as the RMS *Titanic* was designed and built here by the company Harland and Wolff which was set up in the 1860s. Today the company is a leader in ship repair, design and structural engineering, and the shipyards are once again seeing some activity with new plans for development. Harland and Wolff's two yellow cranes known as Samson and Goliath stand as a monument to the great shipbuilding era, but around them a new era has begun. As part of the £1 billion development, the Northern Ireland Science Park and Odyssey complex have already opened and over the next decade or so there are plans for bars, shops, restaurants, marinas, homes and offices.

@ Queen's Island ⓦ www.titanicquarter.com Ⓝ Bus: Laganside
Buscentre or Sightseeing tour bus (see page 61)

CULTURE

Crescent Arts Centre

Housed in a former girls' school, this arts centre hosts
workshops, education/outreach classes, exhibitions and events
from drama, dance and movement to music.
@ 2–4 University Road ⓣ 028 9024 2338 ⓦ www. crescentarts.
org ⓔ info@crescentarts.org ⓛ 10.00–22.00 variable Mon–Fri,
10.00–19.00 variable Sat Ⓝ Bus: 9A-C. Admission charge

King's Hall

This large venue hosts exhibitions, conferences and events from
home, dog and bike shows to concerts and boxing matches.
@ Lisburn Road, Balmoral ⓣ 028 9066 5225
ⓦ www.kingshall.co.uk ⓛ Various Ⓝ Train: Balmoral Station; Bus:
9B/9A to Lisburn Road. Admission charge

Lyric Theatre

Northern Ireland's only full-time producing theatre, featuring a
variety of in-house and touring productions.
@ 55 Ridgeway Street ⓣ 028 9038 5685 ⓦ www.lyrictheatre.
co.uk ⓔ info@lyrictheatre.co.uk ⓛ Various Ⓝ Bus: 7A-B

The Naughton Gallery at Queen's

Located inside Queen's University, this gallery exhibits works
from the university's own collection as well as touring

exhibitions and shows by local and international artists.

🅐 Lanyon Building, Queen's University 🕾 028 9097 3580
🔵 www.naughtongallery.org 🅔 art@naughtongallery.org
🕒 11.00–16.00 Mon–Sat 🔵 Bus: 8A-C

Queen's Film Theatre

Ireland's longest-established cultural cinema, known as the QFT,
screens both classics and contemporary films.

🅐 20 University Square 🕾 028 9097 1097 🔵 www.
queensfilmtheatre.com 🕒 Various 🔵 Bus: 8A-C. Admission charge

Ulster Museum

With 8,000 sq m of galleries, you'll need two or three hours to
get round this museum but it's well worth it. Highlights of the
permanent collection include Palaeolithic bones and Neolithic
ceramics, medieval jewellery and remains of Armada wrecks, Old
Masters and Irish paintings from the 17th century to the
present, sculpture, furniture and fashion, photos and militaria.

🅐 Botanic Gardens 🕾 028 9038 3000 🅕 028 9038 3003
🔵 www.ulstermuseum.org.uk 🕒 10.00–17.00 Mon–Fri, 13.00–17.00
Sat, 14.00–17.00 Sun 🔵 Train: Botanic; Bus: 8A/8B from Donegall
Square East ❶ The museum closed from 2 October 2006 for
approximately 2½ years for major redevelopment.

TAKING A BREAK

Café Vincent £ ❶ Continental-style café serving sandwich and
soup lunches as well as an international menu at dinner.

🅐 78–80 Botanic Avenue 🕾 028 9024 2020 🕒 10.30–22.00 daily

Cargoes £ ❷ Serves coffee and deli foods from feta and olives to pasta and soup. ⓐ 613 Lisburn Road ☎ 028 9066 5451

Clements £ ❸ One of a small chain of coffee bars with seven outlets in Belfast. They pride themselves on their quality coffee and cakes. ⓐ 342 Lisburn Road ☎ 028 9033 1827 ◷ 08.00–00.00 Mon–Thur, 08.00–23.00 Fri, 09.00–23.00 Sat, 10.00–23.00 Sun

Maggie May's Belfast Café £ ❹ This is the place to come for hangover food or if you're just after a good Ulster fry for breakfast. ⓐ 50 Botanic Avenue ☎ 028 9032 2662 ◷ 08.00–22.30 Mon–Sat, 10.00–22.30 Sun

Revelations Internet Café £ ❺ Grab a frappucino, ice cream milkshake or herbal tea and check your email at the same time. ⓐ 27 Shaftesbury Square ☎ 028 9032 0337 ⓦ www.revelations. co.uk ◷ 08.00–22.00 Mon–Fri, 10.00–18.00 Sat, 11.00–19.00 Sun

Ruby Tuesday's £ ❻ Mediterranean-style café with everything from an Ulster fry to pasta and salads. ⓐ 629a Lisburn Road ☎ 028 9066 1220 ◷ 08.15–22.00 Mon–Sat

AFTER DARK

Restaurants
The Blue Print Pizza Company £ ❼ Easy lunch or dinner stop in the heart of the university district with pizzas, pasta and salads. ⓐ 92 Stranmillis Road ☎ 028 9066 3101 ◷ 11.00–23.00 Mon–Sat 13.00–23.00 Sun

Aldens Restaurant ££ ❽ Modern restaurant with a varied menu which attracts local celebrities and politicians. ⓐ 229 Newtownards Road ⓣ 028 9065 0079 ⓦ www.aldensrestaurant.com ⓛ 12.00–14.30 Mon–Fri; 18.00–22.00 Mon–Thur; 18.00–23.00 Fri & Sat

Beatrice Kennedy ££ ❾ One of Belfast's finest restaurants, there's an intimate but relaxed atmosphere here and a modern menu that features the likes of Portavogie crab meat, seared local scallops and rare breed pork loin. ⓐ 44 University Road ⓣ 028 9020 2290 ⓦ www. beatricekennedy.co.uk ⓛ 17.00–22.15 Tues–Sat, 12.30–14.30 & 17.00–20.15 Sun

Four Winds ££ ❿ Venue divided into three parts: the top-floor Ink Restaurant with panoramic city views; slick Blue Glass Wine Bar; and the latest addition, Lounge, a new-age bar. ⓐ 111 Newton Park ⓣ 028 9070 7970 ⓦ www.thefourwinds.co.uk ⓛ Daily – various

Shu Restaurant ££ ⓫ Brasserie-style ground-floor restaurant, basement cocktail and tapas bar with top Belfast DJs on the decks every Wednesday. The head chef is winner of the All-Ireland award. ⓐ 253 Lisburn Road ⓣ 028 9038 655 ⓦ www.shu-restaurant.com ⓛ 12.00–14.30 & 18.00–22.00 Mon–Sat

Cayenne £££ ⓬ Award-winning restaurant owned by celebrity chefs Paul and Jeanne Rankin serving modern Irish cuisine with an international flavour. ⓐ 7 Ascot House, Shaftesbury Square

☎ 028 9033 1532 🌐 www.rankingroup.co.uk 🕐 12.00–14.15
Mon–Fri, 18.00–22.15 Mon–Thur, 18.00–23.15 Fri & Sat,
17.00–20.45 Sun (last reservations)

Clubs & pubs

The Botanic Inn Another favourite pub with three different bars
offering live sports, pub grub, live music and the odd pub quiz.
🅰 23–27 Malone Road ☎ 028 9050 9740 🌐 www.
thebotanicinn.com 🕐 11.30–01.00 Mon–Sat, 12.00–00.00 Sun

Empire Music Hall Legendary venue with a basement pub-style
bar and old theatre-style upper venue with a stage featuring
salsa classes, live music and comedy. 🅰 42 Botanic Avenue ☎ 028
9024 9276 🌐 www.thebelfastempire.com 🕐 08.00–23.00 Mon,
08.00–01.00 Tues–Sat

Lavery's Bar and Gin Palace Golden Mile venue notorious for the
interesting characters that hang out here. A good raucous night
out with food, music, pool hall, DJs and live music.
🅰 Bradbury Place ☎ 028 9087 1106 🌐 www.lavs.co.uk
🕐 12.00–late daily

Madison's Boutique hotel with a café-bar upstairs serving all-
day food, beer and cocktails, with live music on Thursdays, plus
club nights in Club 33 downstairs. 🅰 59–63 Botanic Avenue
☎ 028 9050 9800 🌐 www.madisonshotel.com 🕐 07.00–22.30
daily (Café-bar) Club 33 varies

▶ *Giant's Causeway: a must-see*

OUT OF TOWN
trips

Bangor & County Down

County Down is within easy reach of Belfast city centre. A few miles past George Best City Airport and the horizon widens as you head towards Holywood and Bangor overlooking Belfast Lough, an easy reach for day trips to the beach, country parks and the award-winning Ulster Folk & Transport Museum. South of here is Strangford Lough, with the Ards Peninsular on its east side. A trip to Downpatrick, one of the most important Christian sites in the country and the resting place of Ireland's patron Saint Patrick, is also possible in a day. With a few extra days you could spend some time in the seaside resort of Newcastle, tasting some of the freshest seafood, climbing the peaks of the Mourne Mountains and exploring the Norman castle at Dundrum.

GETTING THERE

There are various routes out of Belfast to County Down by car. For North Down, head out on the A2 past George Best City Airport to Holywood and Bangor or the A20 to Newtownards, which continues along the eastern banks of Strangford Lough to Portaferry. Alternatively you can take the A21/A22 down the west side towards Downpatrick. For Dundrum, Newcastle and the Mourne Mountains go south out of the city along the A24, and for Hillsborough take the M1 and A1.

Trains leave Central Station to Holywood and Bangor. Buses for Newtownards and Portaferry leave from Laganside Buscentre, but for Hillsborough, Downpatrick and Newcastle you'll need to go to Europa Buscentre.

SIGHTS & ATTRACTIONS

Ballyholme Beach

Ballyholme is a small coastal village between Bangor and Groomsport (see page 109), best known for its mile-long sandy beach. It's a favourite with families due to its gentle surf and the nearby nature reserve at Ballymacormick Point.

🅐 Ballyholme Ⓝ Bus: BE4 (from Bangor)

Bangor

Bangor is a large seaside town with plenty of hotels, restaurants and entertainment which is popular with tourists during the summer months. **Bangor Marina** is one of the largest in Northern Ireland. Look out for the rare colony of guillemots nesting in the harbour wall – they're also known as 'Bangor penguins'. Other highlights include: **Bangor Abbey,** a mixture of 15th–19th-century architecture; **Bangor Castle**, an Elizabethan-Jacobean-style mansion that is now actually the Town Hall; and the **Tower House** on Bangor seafront, which was built in 1637 as the Custom House and today houses the tourist information centre.

🅐 Bangor, Down ☎ 028 9146 0081 Bangor Tourist Information
Ⓝ Train: Bangor

Downpatrick

The county town of County Down, Downpatrick is associated with St Patrick, who is buried in the cemetery of **Down Cathedral**, along with St Columba and St Bridget. St Patrick is said to have brought Christianity to Ireland and for this reason this site is considered one of the holiest Christian sites in

Northern Ireland

| 0 | | 20 km |
| 0 | | 10 miles |

ushmills

Whitepark Bay

Rathin Island

Carrick-a-Rede Rope Bridge

Ballintoy

Ballycastle Bay

Giant's Causeway

Ballycastle

Armoy

Cushendun

Ballymoney

Antrim Hills

Cushendall

Clogh

Glencariff Forest Park

Carnlough

The Maidens

Stranraer

Glens of Antrim

Glenarm

M2

Ballygalley Head

Ballymena

Moorfields

Larne

Portmuck

M22

Ballyclare

The Gobbins

M2

Carrickfergus

Antrim

Belfast International ✈

Bangor

Ballyholme Beach

Newtownabbey

Groomsport

Lough Neagh

BELFAST

George Best Belfast City ✈

Ulster Folk Museum

Scrabo Hill Country Park

Newtownards

Lisburn

Comber

Ards Peninsula

M1

Strangford Lough

Sprucefield

Lurgan

Hillsborough

Portavogie

Portadown

Bann

Castle Ward

Portaferry

Banbridge

Inch Abbey

Poyntz Pass

Downpatrick

Castlewellan

Dundrum

Ardglass

Newry

Tollymore Forest Park

852 ▲ Slieve Donard

Newcastle

Dundrum Bay

Mourne Mountains

Glasdrumman

Rostrevor

N

○	City
○	Large Town
○	Small Town
■	POI
	Motorway
	Main Road
	Minor Road
✈	Airport
	Railway

Northern Ireland

Ireland, dating from way before the 19th-century Gothic cathedral that stands here today.

ⓐ English Street ⓣ 028 4461 4922 ⓦ www.downcathedral.org ⓛ 09.30–16.30 Mon–Sat, 14.00–17.00 Sun. Across the car park from the St Patrick Centre (see box) you'll see **Downpatrick Railway**, a historic steam railway that will take you to Inch Abbey. ⓐ Market Street ⓣ 028 4461 5779 ⓦ www.downrail.co.uk ⓛ 13.40–17.00 specific days (see website or call for information). Admission charge. Next to the cathedral, **Down County Museum** is located on the site of a former gaol and military barracks where United Irishman Thomas Russell was hanged in 1803. Today it houses a vast collection of archaeological and historic exhibits from the county.

ⓐ The Mall, English Street ⓣ 028 4461 5218
ⓦ www.downcountymuseum.com ⓛ 10.00–17.00 Mon–Fri, 13.00–17.00 Sat & Sun
ⓐ St Patrick Centre – tourist information
ⓦ www.visitdownpatrick.com ⓝ Bus: Downpatrick

Dundrum Castle

Originally built by John de Courcy in the 12th century, Dundrum is one of the finest Norman castles in Northern Ireland, with panoramic views of Dundrum Bay, the Mourne Mountains and the surrounding countryside. You can climb the round keep.
ⓐ Dundrum Village ⓣ 028 9054 6518 ⓦ www.ehsni.gov.uk
ⓛ 10.00–19.00 Tues–Sat, 14.00–19.00 Sun (Apr–Sept);
10.00–16.00 Sat, 14.00–16.00 Sun (Oct–Mar) ⓝ Bus: Dundrum

Groomsport

A charming seaside village two miles east of Bangor, with a harbour, sandy beach and plenty of pubs and restaurants. Once a fishing village, today it is a popular stop-off for day trippers and sailing enthusiasts.

ⓐ Groomsport ⓝ Bus: 3 (from Bangor)

Hillsborough

Several times winner of the most beautiful village in Northern Ireland prize, Hillsborough doesn't disappoint, with pretty terraced cottages with hanging baskets, boutiques, cafés and pubs selling good grub. Behind the main square you'll find

IRELAND'S PATRON SAINT

Kidnapped from his home in Britain as a teenager, St Patrick spent six years as a slave in County Antrim, before escaping and becoming a missionary, returning to Ireland to convert the Irish to Christianity. According to legend, he taught the Irish people the concept of the trinity using the three-leaved shamrock. At the bottom of Down Hill, where the cathedral stands, is the modern **St Patrick Centre**, where you can learn about the saint's history, browse the souvenirs in the shop and have a cup of tea in the café.

ⓐ 53a Lower Market Street ⓣ 028 4461 9000
ⓦ www.saintpatrickcentre.com ⓛ 10.00–17.00 Mon–Sat (Oct–Mar); 09.30–17.30 Mon–Sat, 13.00–17.30 Sun (Apr, May & Sept); 09.30–18.00 Mon–Sat, 10.00–18.00 Sun (Jun–Aug). Admission charge

Hillsborough Castle, official residence of the Secretary of State for Northern Ireland. Unfortunately it's only open a few days a year. ⓐ Main Street ⓣ 028 9268 2244. Head through the square and downhill and follow signs to **Hillsborough Forest Park** on the left-hand side. ⓐ Tourist Information, The Square, Hillsborough ⓣ 028 9268 9717 ⓝ Bus: Hillsborough

Mourne Mountains

You don't have to be a hard-core hiker to appreciate the Mournes, one of the most stunning spots in Northern Ireland. Drive to Tollymore Forest Park with its gentle woodland strolls or tackle Slieve Donard, Northern Ireland's highest peak. There are plenty of other outdoor activities here from canoeing to orienteering (see pages 35–6).
ⓐ Newcastle ⓦ www.mournemountains.com ⓝ Bus: Newcastle

ⓞ *Cocklerow Cottage at Groomsport*

Newcastle

A popular seaside resort at the foot of the mountains, Newcastle has a sweeping bay looking out to the Irish Sea. It's a good base for exploring the Mourne Mountains, and is home to the Royal County Down golf course.

🄝 Bus: Newcastle

Strangford Lough

Strangford Lough is separated from the Irish Sea by the Ards Peninsula, a strip of land which extends south from Bangor to Portaferry. You can spend more than a day walking along nature trails and visiting all the attractions round the water. **Scrabo Hill Country Park**, northwest of the lough, is dominated by Scrabo Hill and the tower upon it, and there's a picnic site with great views over the lough, 🄐 off the A22/A21 🄣 028 9181 1491 (tower) 🄛 10.30–18.00 (tower). At the southern tip of the lough, make a detour to see **Inch Abbey**, the ruins of a Cistercian abbey founded by John de Courcy in the 12th century. You can take the steam train from nearby **Downpatrick** (see page 105) through scenic countryside. 🄐 off the Downpatrick-Belfast road 🄛 open access all year. Heading east along the A25, you'll come to **Castle Ward**, and an 18th-century country mansion set in beautiful parkland, famous for its opera performances in the summer. 🄐 Strangford 🄣 028 4488 1204 🄛 13.00–18.00 public holidays, school holidays and weekends Mar–Sept (guided tour of house); 10.00–20.00 May–Sept, 10.00–16.00 Oct–Apr (grounds) 🄝 Bus: 16E from Downpatrick to Strangford. From Strangford there's a ferry to and from **Portaferry**. Here the most popular attraction is **Exploris**, an aquarium with species native to the shores of

Northern Ireland, including bass, edible sea urchin, octopus and peacock worm.

ⓐ The Rope Walk, Castle Street, Portaferry ⓣ 028 4272 8062
ⓦ www.exploris.org.uk ⓛ 10.00–18.00 Mon–Fri, 11.00–18.00 Sat, 12.00–18.00 Sun (Apr–Aug); 10.00–17.00 Mon–Fri, 11.00–17.00 Sat, 13.00–17.00 Sun (Sept–Mar).

CULTURE

Ulster Folk & Transport Museum

One of the most popular attractions in Northern Ireland, this museum is set in over 170 acres of countryside. The Folk Museum comprises buildings from all over the province transported here, rebuilt and restored to give an authentic view of life in early 20th-century Ulster. In each cottage, mill and shop you'll meet 'residents' in period costume spinning at the wheel, cooking soda wheaten over the fire or serving behind the counter. The Transport Museum has a comprehensive display from horse-drawn carts to Irish-built motor cars, locomotives and the history of ship and aircraft building. You'll need a full day to get round the whole lot so bring a picnic, snack in the tea rooms or head to Cultra Manor for the Sunday carvery.

ⓐ 153 Bangor Road, Cultra, Holywood ⓣ 028 9042 8428
ⓦ www.uftm.org.uk ⓔ uftm.info@magni.org.uk ⓛ 10.00–17.00 Mon–Fri, 10.00–18.00 Sat, 11.00–18.00 Sun (Mar–Jun); 10.00–18.00 Mon–Sat, 11.00–18.00 Sun (Jul–Sept); 10.00–16.00 Mon–Fri, 10.00–17.00 Sat, 11.00–17.00 Sun (Oct–Feb) ⓝ Bus: Museum entrance; Train: Cultra Halt. Admission charge

TAKING A BREAK

Restaurants

Mario's Restaurant ££ As Italian restaurants go, this is just about as authentic as you can get and has great views over Dundrum

◗ *Bangor Marina*

Bay. Chef and owner Mario sources his fresh produce locally and his staff have been with him for years – you'll definitely get a warm welcome here. **ⓐ** 65 South Promenade, Newcastle **ⓣ** 028 4372 3912 **ⓛ** 18.00–21.30 last orders Mon–Sat, 12.00–14.30, 17.00–21.00 Sun

Mourne Seafood Bar ££ Some of the freshest seafood and fish dishes on the coast here. They even have their own mussel and oyster beds in Carlingford Lough and sell fresh fish to take home. During the week there's a two-course set price lunch. **ⓐ** 77 Main Street, Dundrum **ⓣ** 028 4375 1377 **ⓦ** www. mourneseafood.com **ⓛ** 12.00–21.00 Mon–Fri, closes Mon & Tues off-season

Restaurant 1614 ££ Located in Ireland's oldest coaching inn, this restaurant serves a combination of classical and modern cuisine. Also offers a set price bistro menu for two. **ⓐ** The Old Inn, Main Street, Crawfordsburn **ⓣ** 028 9185 3255 **ⓦ** www. theoldinn.com **ⓛ** 19.00–21.30 Mon–Sat, 12.30–14.30 Sun

Mitre Restaurant £££ Considered to be one of the best restaurants in Northern Ireland, with a fine dining set menu. **ⓐ** Culloden Hotel, Bangor Road, Holywood **ⓣ** 028 9042 6777 **ⓦ** www.hastingshotels.com **ⓛ** 19.00–21.30 Mon–Sat, 12.30–14.30 & 19.00–20.45 Sun

ACCOMMODATION

Hotels and Guest Houses
Tara Guest House £ Traditional town house with spacious rooms

and views of Bangor Marina. **a** 51 Princetown Road, Bangor
t 028 9146 8820 **w** www.taraguesthouse.co.uk

Royal Hotel ££ Family-run hotel on Bangor seafront with café,
bar and restaurant. **a** 26–28 Quay Street, Bangor **t** 028 9127
1866 **w** www.royalhotelbangor.com

The Old Inn £££ Located in Ireland's oldest coaching inn, famous
guests are said to include the highwayman Dick Turpin and
former US President George Bush (senior). Stay in cosy rooms
with four-poster beds. **a** Main Street, Crawfordsburn
w www.theoldinn.com **t** 028 9185 3255

Slieve Donard £££ Impressive Victorian hotel and Newcastle's
finest with views of the Mourne Mountains and the Irish Sea
plus a luxury spa, restaurant with fine Irish cuisine and hotel bar
with live entertainment. **a** Downs Road, Newcastle **t** 028 4372
1066 **w** www.hastingshotels.com

Camping and hostels
Newcastle Hostel £ Located right on the seafront near pubs and
restaurants. **a** 30 Downs Road **t** 028 4372 2133

Windsor Caravan Park £ One of many caravan parks along the
Dundrum Road, this one permits touring caravans and has hire
facilities. **a** A2 from Newcastle to Dundrum **t** 028 4372 3367

Antrim Coast

The Antrim Coast is one of the most beautiful parts of Northern Ireland. A stunning coastline of lush forest glens, sweeping bays, and turquoise seas during the summer, in the winter it is wild and romantic. Steeped in myth and legend with a history of settlement dating way back to the Neolithic era, there are many natural and man-made sights, including Giant's Causeway, Bushmills Distillery, Dunluce Castle, Carrick-a-Rede Rope Bridge, Rathlin Island and the spectacular drive along the coast, as well as picture-box villages such as Cushendun and Ballintoy and seaside towns at Ballycastle and Portrush.

GETTING THERE

Hiring a car gives you the freedom to explore the Antrim Coast at your leisure. Drive north out of Belfast along the M2, then take the M5 towards Carrickfergus (about 20 minutes from the city centre). From there take the A2 coast road. Ballintoy, Carrick-a-Rede, Giant's Causeway, and Bushmills are all within two hours' drive, with Portrush a further 15 minutes away. Ulsterbus run the Antrim Coaster from Laganside Buscentre to Portrush and Coleraine via the coast road. There are trains from Belfast Central Station to Coleraine, where you can pick up another train or bus to your destination. Caledonian MacBrayne run around six ferries a day from Ballycastle to Rathlin Island during the summer months.
🕿 028 2076 9299 🌐 www.calmac.co.uk

SIGHTS & ATTRACTIONS

Antrim Coast Road

The drive along the coastal road is breathtaking, with its craggy cliffs, pretty bays, glens and picturesque villages. You can drive along the coast on the A2 from Larne to Ballycastle, continuing along the coastal road after Cushendall or going cross-country to explore the Glens. Cushendall and Cushendun are among the prettiest villages.

ⓐ A2 Antrim Coast Road ⓝ Bus: Antrim Coaster (252), drive or tour

Bushmills Distillery

The oldest licensed whiskey distillery in the world, with a history dating back to 1608. You can take a tour round the distillery but it can get very busy; tickets are sold on a first-come, first-served basis.

ⓐ Main Street, Bushmills ⓣ 028 2073 1521
ⓦ www.bushmills.com ⓛ 09.30–17.00 Mon–Sat, 12.00–17.30 Sun (Apr–Oct) last tour 16.00 each day; 10.30. 11.30, 13.30, 14.30, 15.30 Mon–Fri, 13.30, 14.30, 15.30 Sat & Sun (Nov–Mar) ⓝ Bus: Bushmills. Admission charge

Carrick-a-Rede Rope Bridge

Fight your fear of heights and take the challenge of walking across this rope bridge. Actually it is much better than the original, which only had a single handrail. It was constructed by fishermen who wanted to cross to the rocky island to fish for salmon, but it was eventually taken over by the National Trust,

which added the much safer bridge seen here today. Some people make it over to the other side only to panic and not be able to return – until the wardens tell them they will be winched up into a helicopter and then presented with the bill!

🄰 Whitepark Bay Road, Ballintoy 🄣 028 2076 9839

🅦 www.nationaltrust.org.uk

🄴 carrickarede@nationaltrust.org.uk. Admission charge

Carrickfergus Castle

A dominant feature of the coastal town of Carrickfergus and the site of many a battle, the castle has a colourful history dating back 800 years. The English retreated here during Edward the Bruce's invasion and during the 14th century it fell to the Scots after a long siege. Over the years it has been used as a prison, a magazine, an armoury and an air-raid shelter.

🔺 *The hair-raising Carrick-a-Rede Rope Bridge*

(a) Marine Highway (t) 028 9335 1273 (w) www.ehsni.org.uk
(l) 10.00–16.00 Mon–Sat, 14.00–16.00 Sun (Jan–Mar);
10.00–18.00 Mon–Sat, 14.00–18.00 Sun (Apr–Dec)
(n) Train: Carrickfergus. Admission charge

Dunluce Castle

The ruins of this medieval castle perch on the edge of the North
Antrim cliffs between Bushmills and Portrush. During a storm in
1639, a whole section of the castle collapsed into the sea, killing
the cooks and kitchen staff. The castle was abandoned and over
time the entire building fell into disrepair. There's a visitor centre
and shop, and tours round the castle.
(a) A2 Coast Road between Bushmills and Portrush (t) 028 2073
1938 (f) 028 2073 2850 (e) dunluce.castle@doeni.gov.uk
(l) 10.00–16.00 daily (Oct–Mar); 10.00–17.00 daily (Apr–Sept)
(n) Drive or tour bus only. Admission charge

Giant's Causeway

A must-see for anyone visiting the province, Giant's Causeway is
one of Northern Ireland's top attractions and a UNESCO World
Heritage Site. Until geologists came up with scientific theories on
the origins of the strange hexagonal basalt columns, the area was
steeped in myth and legend. The most famous story surrounds
Fionn McCumhaill (McCool), a giant who fell in love with a
Scottish belle and created a pathway to reach her. In reality, it's
thought to have been the result of volcanic eruptions and the
subsequent cooling of the lava by the sea. In total there are
around 40,000 columns of varying heights. Look out for the
Giant's Boot, Organ, Chimney Stack and Camel's Back, among

▲ *Romantic Dunluce Castle*

other features. You can walk the route from the visitor centre down to the Causeway and ascend the cliffs, returning along the top. Alternatively there is a bus that will take you to and from the main site.

ⓐ Two miles east of Bushmills ❶ 028 2073 1855 (visitor centre)
❶ 028 2073 1582 (National Trust) ⓦ www.nationaltrust.org.uk
ⓔ giantscauseway@nationaltrust.org.uk ❶ 10.00–17.00 daily
ⓝ Train: Belfast Bridge Street to Giant's Causeway The Nook Main. Admission charge

Giant's Causeway & Bushmills Railway

Running on the route of the original Causeway Tram, which closed in 1949, the line re-opened in 2002. Riding the narrow-gauge steam train is a great way to travel between the two attractions. There are picnic areas, toilets, café and car park at the Giant's Causeway Station. A service is usually run during St Patrick's weekend, Easter, weekends from Easter until June, daily during July and August and weekends during September and October.

ⓐ Runkerry Road, Bushmills ❶ 028 2073 2844. Admission charge

Nine Glens of Antrim – Glenarm, Glencloy, Glenariff, Glenballyemon, Glenaan, Glencorp, Glendun, Glenshesk and Glentaisie

From the Antrim plateau to the Antrim Coast road, the nine green Glens of Antrim are a rich mix of waterfalls, rivers, lush forests, peat bogs, flora and fauna. Glenariff Forest Park is one of the most beautiful areas, with trails leading past scenic mountain viewpoints.

ⓐ Antrim Coast ⓝ Bus: Antrim Coaster; Car: A2

THE GLENS OF ANTRIM: LAND OF MYTHS

Many legends have circulated the Glens of Antrim, from the Giant Fionn McCool to the Children of Lir (who were turned into swans by their evil stepmother Aiofe). Make a detour from the Glenariff Forest Park to visit Slemish Mountain, where St Patrick is said to have tended Miliucc's sheep after he was captured and brought to Ireland. Watch out for the Watershee, a female fairy who is said to sing sweet songs to lure travellers into lakes and bogs before drowning them. And remember, never cut down a hawthorn tree or you'll upset the fairy folk and bad luck will surely follow. Whether you believe it or not, you'll find magical scenery and plenty of birdwatching, fishing and hiking.

Portrush

A favourite holiday destination, Portrush is set in a wide sweeping bay with sandy beaches. Local attractions include Waterworld indoor water facility, Barry's Amusements (largest amusement park in Ireland) and the Countryside Centre (interactive marine exhibits). There's also surfing on the Blue Flag beaches, fishing on or off shore, tennis, bowling, golf at Royal Portrush, and coastal walking and cycling routes.

ⓐ North Antrim Coast ⓝ Bus: Dunluce Avenue

Rathlin Island

Located six miles offshore from Ballycastle, Rathlin Island is eight miles long and less than a mile wide. A birdwatchers' paradise, this is home to Northern Ireland's largest seabird colony – look out for razorbills, fulmars and puffins from the RSPB viewpoint at the West Light. This is just one of three lighthouses on the island, as the wild coastline has led to numerous shipwrecks over the years (about 40).

ⓐ Six miles off Ballycastle ⓣ 028 7032 7960 or 0774 556 6924 Paul Quinn for tours ⓦ Ferry: Ballycastle to Rathlin Island

Whitepark Bay & Ballintoy

This beautiful sweeping bay runs between Portbradden and Ballintoy and is one of the most popular walking routes in the area. The path winds along the basalt cliff top. Ballintoy itself is a picturesque village with its iconic white church and a limestone harbour sheltered by the cliffs behind.

ⓐ North Antrim Coast ⓦ Bus: Ballintoy

FESTIVALS

Some of the best festivals during the year include: **Coleraine Community and Arts Festival** with a programme of cultural activities and music (late June); **Larne Alive Festival**, a month-long event with music, train rides, steam engines and circus acts; **Feis na Gleann**, a traditional Irish music festival throughout the glens (June); **Ballycastle Fleadh**, a weekend of traditional song and dance (June); **Medieval Lughnasa Fayre** in Carrickfergus with costumed performers (July); **Heart of the Glens Festival** in Cushendall with local singing and dance (August); and the **Ould Lammas Fair** in Ballycastle, one of the oldest in Ireland with livestock sales and stalls selling *dulse*, dried edible seaweed, and *yelloman*, a very sugary candy not unlike rock.

TAKING A BREAK

Many of the accommodation options below also have restaurants but there are cafés and bars in every village along the Antrim Coast Road serving both lunch and dinner. Cushendall and Cushendun are among the prettiest villages, but there's more choice in places like Carrickfergus, Larne, Ballycastle and Portrush. Some of the main attractions, such as Giant's Causeway and Carrick-a-Rede Rope Bridge have cafés where you can stop for refreshments.

AFTER DARK

Restaurants & Bars

55° North £ Split-level family restaurant overlooking the sea which serves a wide range of contemporary dishes, from risotto of pan-seared scallops to braised lamb. ❸ 1 Causeway Street, Portrush ❶ 028 7082 2811 ⓦ www.55-north.com ❹ 12.30–14.00 & 17.30–21.00 Tues–Thur, 12.15–14.15 & 17.00–21.00 Fri, 12.00–14.30 & 17.00–21.00 Sat, 17.00–20.00 Sun (opens later during peak summer months)

Central Bar £ Restored traditional bar dating back to 1861 with traditional music on Wednesdays and live bands at the weekends. Plans to start selling pub grub soon. ❸ 12 Ann Street, Ballycastle ❶ 028 2076 3877 ❷ centralbar@btinternet.com ❹ 11.30–23.30 daily

The Distillers Arms £ Comfy pub in Bushmills where you can stop for a pint in front of the fire with lunch or dinner menus including seafood chowder, fish and chips and home-cured Irish salmon. ⓐ Main Street ⓣ 028 2073 1044 ⓦ www.distillersarms.com ⓛ 12.30–15.00 & 17.00–21.00 daily for food, pub open till the last one leaves (summer season); 17.30–21.00 Wed–Sat, 12.30–15.00 Sat & Sun, pub opens 17.00 Mon–Fri, 11.00 Sat & Sun (winter season)

The Manor House £ A former Georgian gentleman's house, today it is a guesthouse and restaurant serving fresh fish. Dinner should be pre-ordered. ⓐ Rathlin Island ⓣ 028 2076 3964 ⓦ www.nationaltrust.org ⓛ dinner served at 19.00

The Nook at the Giant's Causeway ££ Housed in a former 1850s schoolhouse, this restaurant offers a taste of Ulster and is renowned for its scones. ⓐ 48 Causeway Road ⓣ 028 2073 2993 ⓛ 10.30–20.00 restaurant; until 22.00 bar (summer – closes earlier in winter)

ACCOMMODATION

Hotels and Guesthouses
Ahimsa £ B&B in a modernised cottage with a vegetarian restaurant and organic garden. You can even request a session of yoga and reflexology. ⓐ 243 Whitepark Road, Bushmills ⓣ 028 2073 1383 ⓔ Sheila.reynolds@btopenworld.com

The Burn £ Comfortable B&B in picturesque Cushendall. ⓐ 63 Ballyeamon Road, Cushendall ⓣ 028 2177 1733 ⓦ www.theburn-guesthouse.com ⓔ theburn63@hotmail.com

Causeway Hotel ££ B&B-style accommodation located right on the doorstep of Giant's Causeway, with superb views. ⓐ 40 Causeway Road, Bushmills ⓣ 028 2073 1210 ⓕ 028 2073 2552 ⓦ www.giants-causeway-hotel.com

Smugglers Inn ££ B&B near Giant's Causeway with a restaurant and bar. ⓐ 306 Whitepark Road ⓣ 028 2073 1577 ⓦ www.smugglers-inn.co.uk ⓔ jenny@smugglers-inn.co.uk

The Marine Hotel £££ Comfortable hotel overlooking Ballycastle's new harbour and marina, with restaurant, bar and entertainment. ⓐ 1 North Street, Ballycastle ⓣ 028 2076 2222 ⓦ www.marinehotel.net ⓔ info@marinehotel.com

Camping and hostels
Cushendall Caravan Park £ Camping on the Antrim Coast road. ⓐ 62 Coast Road, Cushendall ⓣ 028 2177 1699

Mill Rest Youth Hostel £ Cheap and basic accommodation for those on a budget. ⓐ 49 Main Street, Bushmills ⓣ 028 2076 3612

▶ *Belfast Welcome Centre: find out all you need to know*

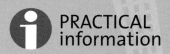

PRACTICAL
information

Directory

GETTING THERE

By air

BMI Baby operates several flights a day between Belfast International Airport and Birmingham, Cardiff, Manchester and Nottingham East Midlands, and between George Best Belfast City Airport and London Heathrow. **easyJet** operates several flights a day between Belfast International and Bristol, Edinburgh, Glasgow, Liverpool, London (Gatwick, Luton and Stansted) and Newcastle, and on Monday, Wednesday, Friday and Sunday to and from Inverness. **Jet2.com** operates daily flights between Belfast International, Blackpool and Leeds Bradford. **Manx2.com** operates two flights during the week, one at weekends between Belfast International and the Isle of Man, and one a day to and from Blackpool. **British Airways** operates several flights a day between George Best Belfast City Airport and Manchester. **British Northwest** operates several flights a day between Belfast City and Blackpool via the Isle of Man. **EuroManx** operates flights every day between Belfast City and the Isle of Man. **Air Berlin** operates several flights a day between Belfast City and London Stansted. **Flybe** operates several flights a day between Belfast City and Aberdeen, Birmingham, Doncaster Sheffield, Edinburgh, Exeter, Glasgow, Guernsey, Leeds Bradford, Liverpool, London Gatwick, Manchester, Newcastle and Southampton, and one a day to and from Bristol and Jersey.

Air Berlin ☎ 0870 738 8880 ⓦ www.airberlin.com
BMI Baby ☎ 08702 642229 ⓦ www.bmibaby.com

British Airways ⓣ 0870 850 9850 Ⓦ www.ba.com
British Northwest ⓣ 0800 083 7783 Ⓦ www.flybnwa.co.uk
easyJet ⓣ 0871 244 2366 Ⓦ www.easyjet.com
EuroManx ⓣ 0870 787 7879 Ⓦ www.euromanx.com
Flybe ⓣ 0871 700 0535 Ⓦ www.flybe.com
Jet2.com ⓣ 0871 226 1737 Ⓦ www.jet2.com
Manx2.com ⓣ 0870 242 2226 Ⓦ www.manx2.com

Many people are aware that air travel emits CO_2, which contributes to climate change. You may be interested in the possibility of lessening the environmental impact of your flight through the charity Climate Care, which offsets your CO_2 by funding environmental projects around the world. Visit Ⓦ www.climatecare.org

By rail
Services to Belfast run from Bangor, Derry City and Portrush, Larne and Portadown. There's also the cross-border Enterprise service with Iarnród Éireann eight times a day between Belfast and Dublin with main Northern Ireland stops at Derry, Coleraine, Belfast Central, Lisburn, Portadown and Newry.

By ferry
Stena Line operates regular Belfast–Stranraer, Belfast–Troon and Larne (north of Belfast)–Fleetwood services, Ⓦ www.stenaline.co.uk. Steam Packet operates a Belfast–Douglas (Isle of Man) service, Ⓦ www.steam-packet.com. P&O Irish Sea Ferries operates Larne–Troon and Larne–Cairnryan services, Ⓦ www.poirishsea.com. Norfolkline

Irish Sea operates a Belfast–Liverpool service,
ⓦ www.norfolkline-ferries.co.uk.

By coach
Scottish Citylink runs services between Belfast's Europa
Buscentre and various Scottish cities,
ⓦ www.citylinkonlinesales.com. National Express runs services
between the Europa Buscentre and several English and Welsh
cities, ⓦ www.nationalexpress.com.

By car
Belfast is approximately 70 miles from Derry by A roads and the
M2 motorway, 100 miles from Dublin and 262 miles from Cork
on toll-paying motorways, A roads and the M1 motorway into
Belfast city centre. There are several ferry routes from the rest of
the UK that come into Belfast ferry port close to the city centre
and Larne (23 miles north of Belfast).

ENTRY FORMALITIES
Citizens of the rest of the UK need some form of photographic
ID (usually a valid passport or driving licence). Citizens of EU
countries, USA, Canada, Australia, New Zealand and South Africa
do not require a visa if coming to Northern Ireland (or the rest of
the UK) as a visitor.

Visitors to the UK and Northern Ireland are entitled to bring
the following duty paid goods into the country for their own
personal use: up to 3,200 cigarettes, 400 cigarillos, 200 cigars,
3 kg of smoking tobacco, 10 litres of spirits, 90 litres of wine
(60 litres of sparkling wine), 20 litres of fortified wine and 110

litres of beer. However, if you are questioned by Customs officials and cannot satisfy them that it is not for commercial use, it could be seized and not returned. Exceptions apply to the following EU countries: from Czech Republic, 200 cigarettes or 250 g of smoking tobacco or 50 cigars or 100 cigarillos; from Estonia, 200 cigarettes or 250 g of smoking tobacco (no restrictions on other tobacco products if for your own use); from Hungary, Latvia, Lithuania, Poland, Slovakia and Slovenia, 200 cigarettes (no restrictions on other tobacco products if for your own use).

If you are travelling from non-EU countries you have a duty free allowance of 200 cigarettes or 100 cigarillos or 50 cigars or 250 g of tobacco; 2 litres of still table wine; 1 litre of spirits or strong liqueurs over 22% volume or 2 litres of fortified wine, sparkling wine or other liqueurs; 60 cc/ml of perfume; 250 cc/ml of toilet water and £145 worth of all other goods including gifts and souvenirs.

MONEY

As with the rest of the UK, in Northern Ireland the currency is UK pounds sterling. Northern Ireland has four clearing banks – Bank of Ireland, First Trust, Northern Bank and Ulster Bank, which print their own bank notes. These are valid sterling notes in the same denominations as the rest of the UK (£5, £10, £20 and £50) but it's advisable to change them to English notes if you're moving on to England as many places don't like to accept them, despite their legality. Most banks have ATMs and are located throughout the city centre, main commercial areas of the city and all towns throughout the province. Larger banks in

Belfast have Bureaux de Change, but you can also try travel agencies, the Belfast Welcome Centre, some Tourist Information Centres, large hotels and some tourist attractions.

Credit cards are generally accepted in most shops, restaurants, bars and attractions, but if there's any doubt, it is best to check first to avoid any embarrassment.

HEALTH, SAFETY & CRIME

There should be absolutely no problem with the drinking water in Belfast – the main supply comes from the Mourne Mountains to the city. Likewise, there should be no problem with the city's food.

The public health-care system in Northern Ireland is part of the UK National Health Service (NHS) but here it integrates both health and social care into one system, so citizens of the UK are covered for health care. As part of a reciprocal agreement, citizens of the EU are entitled to reduced-cost and sometimes free medical treatment if they have a European Health Insurance Card (EHIC). You can apply for this in your country of citizenship. Make sure you have ID with you as well as your EHIC.

As this may not cover all your medical needs, it is always better have your own private travel insurance to pay for repatriation, should you need it. Insurance also usually covers you if you are a victim of crime, but check your policy carefully before you travel.

Northern Ireland has the second lowest crime rate in Europe. Even during The Troubles tourists were rarely targeted or directly affected. Just use your common sense as you would

when travelling anywhere – don't take too much cash out with you, don't flash expensive jewellery around or walk along the street with a big open map. It can also get quite rowdy at the weekends along the Golden Mile and Botanic but most people are just happy after a few drinks. However, if you're lost or feel uncomfortable it's better to ask someone for directions during the day – most people are happy to help – or take a taxi home if it's late, Fon A Cab ☎ 028 9023 3333. If you do have an emergency, call the **police, ambulance or fire service** on **999**. For lost valuables call the PSNI (Police Service of Northern Ireland) **Police Lost Property** on 028 9065 0222. Alternatively you can call into Musgrave Police Station on Ann Street (by Queen's Bridge) for this or other matters.

⬤ *The city centre is easy to navigate*

OPENING HOURS

Shops usually open from Monday to Saturday 09.30–17.30 with late-night shopping on Thursday (21.00). Larger stores and most high-street stores in Belfast city centre also open on Sunday from 13.00–18.00. Banks generally open from Monday to Friday 09.30–16.30 but some also open on Saturday mornings. They are always closed on Sundays and public holidays.

TOILETS

There are several public toilets in the city centre either as standalones in the street or in car parks, bus stations (Europa and Laganside Buscentres), shopping centres and markets, including CastleCourt on Royal Avenue. You can also find clean toilets in department stores and museums, and McDonald's in Royal Avenue is also widely used, although it's not the cleanest of places. In an emergency you can also go in to pubs and cafés, but you usually have to buy something.

CHILDREN

Children are welcomed and allowed in more establishments than England, but in general they are not allowed in bars and pubs, unless they serve food as well. Children should love going on sightseeing bus tours, boat trips and to the Odyssey Centre. They'll also enjoy Belfast Zoo and even the Castle and Ulster Museum. There's often entertainment in Custom House Square that they'll find fun.

- **Sightseeing Bus Tours** Might not be so much fun for very young ones but most children enjoy just riding a bus (see page 61).

- **Odyssey Centre** There's all-day entertainment here for the kids, including the W5 interactive discovery centre and the Pavilion with IMAX cinema and restaurants (see page 94)

- **Belfast Castle and Cave Hill Country Park** If there aren't any events on at the castle you can have a look around, then take the kids on a nature trail through Cave Hill Country Park up to Napoleon's Nose, see page 82

- **Titanic Boat Tours** Kids can discover something about the Titanic and enjoy the short boat trip at the same time (see page 96).

COMMUNICATIONS

Phones

Coin- and card-operated telephone booths can be found all over the city. Phone cards can be purchased at tobacconists and supermarkets. All phones can be used to call abroad – it's cheaper before 08.00, after 18.00 and at weekends. To call the UK you just need to dial the area code and the number. To phone anywhere else you should dial the national code first (353 Republic of Ireland, 1 USA or Canada, 61 Australia, 64 New Zealand, 72 South Africa) plus the area code (minus the 0 if there is one) and the rest of the number. For international operator assistance call 155.

The Belfast and other Northern Ireland numbers in this book include the Northern Ireland number (028) followed by an area code and a six-digit number. Within Northern Ireland you don't need to dial 028 but you do need to dial the rest of the digits.

Post

Post offices are generally open from 09.00–17.30 Monday–Friday and 09.00–12.00 on Saturday. The main post office in Belfast city centre is at Castle Junction. You can post your letters at post offices or in the red post boxes around the city and the rest of Northern Ireland. Stamps can be bought at post offices, tobacconists, supermarkets and some tourist offices and petrol stations.

Internet

You can access the Internet from the Belfast Welcome Centre and Revelations Internet Café in Shaftesbury Square. There may also be internet access in your hotel.

ELECTRICITY

As with the rest of the UK and Republic of Ireland, the current is 240V (50Hz) and three-pin plugs are used. Visitors from outside the UK or Ireland will need an adaptor.

TRAVELLERS WITH DISABILITIES

To stay in line with EU regulations, facilities are being improved in Northern Ireland as with the rest of the UK. Work on some venues has already taken place (Grand Opera House and large hotels and restaurants), providing wheelchair access via ramps or lifts. Sources of advice for travellers with disabilities include:

Shopmobility Belfast ⓐ Westgate House, 2 Queen Street, Belfast ⓣ 028 9080 8090 ⓦ www.shopmobilitybelfast.com

Disability Action ⓣ 028 9049 1011 ⓦ www.disabilityaction.org

FURTHER INFORMATION

Belfast has a very helpful tourist office in the city centre as well as two at Belfast International and George Best Belfast City Airport.

Belfast & Northern Ireland Welcome Centre ⓐ 47 Donegall Place
ⓣ 028 9024 6609 ⓕ 028 9031 2424 ⓔ info@belfastvisitor.com
ⓛ 09.00–17.30 Mon–Sat (Oct–May); 09.00–19.00 Mon–Sat, 12.00–17.00 Sun (June–Sept)

Useful websites include the official tourism website for Belfast, ⓦ www.gotobelfast.com and
ⓦ www.discovernorthernireland.com

BACKGROUND READING

Made in Belfast by Vivienne Pollock and Trevor Parkhill gives a good overview of life, work and industry, from the linen mills and shipbuilding to entertainments, with plenty of old photographs to illustrate. For more information on the building of the Titanic see *Building the Titanic: An Epic Tale of Modern Engineering and Human Endeavour* by Rod Green. *Belfast and the Irish Language* is a collection of essays on Belfast's relationship with the Irish language from its earliest roots to the present. *War as a Way of Life* by John Conroy gives a more intimate view on growing up in West Belfast, while *The Wee Wild One: Stories of Belfast and Beyond* by Ruth C Schwertfiger gives a fresh view on the city through literature and strange tales.

Emergencies

EMERGENCY NUMBERS

Ambulance and all-purpose number for emergencies **999**

MEDICAL EMERGENCIES

Only call 999 in an absolute emergency. If you can, ask a pharmacist for help or visit a doctor's surgery. In case of emergency you should ask to be taken to the nearest hospital. The Royal has a specialist hospital just for children, as well as maternity and dentistry hospitals. Citizens of the UK are entitled to full medical treatment and holders of EHIC cards (see page 132) are entitled to basic medical treatment. Still, travel insurance with a good level of medical cover is advisable for repatriation and essential for non-EU visitors.

Emergency medical services are very good in Northern Ireland and often the waiting time in Accident and Emergency is less than in other parts of the UK. You should try and provide as much information as possible about the patient, including personal details and the symptoms. If you are physically able, go to A&E (Accident and Emergency) at the nearest hospital or ask the hotel or pharmacist for the number of a local doctor, clinic or dentist.

Belfast City Hospital ⓐ 51 Lisburn Road ⓣ 028 9032 9241
Mater Hospital Trust ⓐ 45–51 Crumlin Road ⓣ 028 9074 1211
Royal Victoria Hospital ⓐ 274 Grosvenor Road ⓣ 028 9024 0503
Shaftesbury Square Hospital ⓐ 116–120 Great Victoria Street
ⓣ 028 9032 9808

POLICE

If you are unlucky enough to be the victim of crime, you should call the PSNI (Police Service of Northern Ireland). Only call 999 in absolute emergencies, otherwise contact the police station directly on foot or by phone. If you lose some property or have something stolen then you should report this to the lost property office at Musgrave Police Station. You'll be given an official report to help make any necessary insurance claims. It is advisable to take some photographic ID with you when you make the report.

Musgrave Police Station ⓐ Ann Street ⓣ 028 9065 7888 (Lost Property)

CONSULATES & EMBASSIES

Australian High Commission ⓐ Australia House, Strand, London WC28 4LA ⓣ 020 7379 4334

Canadian Consulate ⓐ Unit 3, Ormeau Business Park ⓣ/ⓕ 028 9127 2060

New Zealand Honorary Consul ⓐ 118a Lisburn Road, Crumlin ⓣ 028 9264 8098

South African High Commission ⓣ 020 7925 8900 ⓕ 020 7925 8930

US Consulate ⓐ Danesfort House, 223 Stranmillis Road ⓣ 028 9038 6100 ⓕ 028 9068 1301

The publishers would like to thank Christopher Holt for supplying his copyright photographs for this book. Supplementary photographs on pages 10 and 34 are © Belfast Tourist Office; on page 21 © Waterfront Hall and page 28 © Apartment.

Copy editor: Rebecca McKie
Proofreader: Ali Rasch

Send your thoughts to
books@thomascook.com

- Found a great bar, club, shop or must-see sight that we don't feature?

- Like to tip us off about any information that needs updating?

- Want to tell us what you love about this handy little guidebook and more importantly how we can make it even handier?

Then here's your chance to tell all! Send us ideas, discoveries and recommendations today and then look out for your valuable input in the next edition of this title. As an extra 'thank you' from Thomas Cook Publishing, you'll be automatically entered into our exciting prize draw.

Send an email to the above address (stating the book's title) or write to: CitySpots Project Editor, Thomas Cook Publishing, PO Box 227, The Thomas Cook Business Park, Unit 18, Coningsby Road, Peterborough PE3 8SB, UK.